D1598860

Fort Apache Bronx, NY

(Life at the 41st Precinct)

by
Tom Walker

Copyright © 2000
by J. & B. Gould
Printed in the USA

Published by
J.B.L. Publications, Inc.
Distributed by Gould Publications, Inc.
1333 North US Highway 17–92
Longwood, FL 32750–3724
(800) 717–7917
http://www.gouldlaw.com

First published in 1976.

ISBN: 0-87526-577-4   **tw**

While the events in this work are true, the names have been changed out of respect for the privacy of the individuals. The views expressed here are the author's.

Library of Congress Cataloging in Publication Data

Walker, Thomas, 1935–
    Fort Apache.

Autobiographical.
I. Walker, Thomas, 1935–   1. Title

To the men and women of the Forty-first Precinct, past and present, without whom this book would have been impossible.

Once upon a time in the awe-inspiring city of New York there existed in the verdant borough of the Bronx a square mile police precinct that rivaled the legendary intrigue of the Casbah, that made Dodge City and Tombstone appear to be family towns, a place that found its only equal in the grassy plains of Custer's last stand, a precinct that came to be affectionately known to the four-hundred police officers who manned this historic and tiny outpost as "Fort Apache".

That was over thirty years ago. The anarchy of the 60's was in full bloom. Militant groups of various descriptions were violently trying to bring the government to its knees. The police, the most visible and vulnerable instrument of that government, were the prime targets of their terrorist attacks. Fort Apache became their sanctuary, a place to hide amid the chaos and mayhem that prevailed on those mean South Bronx streets.

A few years later as the city slowly demolished the burned-out skeletons of guttered tenement houses, the precinct would be re-named, "The Little House on the Prairie." Peace had finally come to Fort Apache, but the human costs to both the inhabitants of those tenements and the police officers who valiantly struggled to protect both themselves and the newcomers who populated those buildings were of tragic proportions.

In my time at Fort Apache, the Four-one precinct averaged over 100 murders a year, it led the city in rapes, robberies and assaults. Vicious gangs preyed upon the overwhelmingly decent and hard-working immigrants who were trying to establish themselves in their new homeland. While arsonists burned the tenements, the police had to protect the courageous firefighters as they tried to save the lives of sleeping inhabitants. It was indeed hell on earth.

Fort Apache's police officers constantly came under hostile and deadly fire – two officers were killed during my tour there. In one year we had 35 shootouts with an emboldened and ruthless criminal element. Numerous officers were seriously wounded, maimed for life and forced into retirement. Fort Apache justly deserved its infamous reputation as the most violent precinct in New York City history. Now over 30 years later, things have changed dramatically for the better. I visited the precinct last year to speak at a Community Council breakfast.

Fort Apache is no more. The Little House on the Prairie is no more. There were only 4 murders in the Four-one precinct last year and the area has been handsomely rebuilt. As I rode those memory-filled streets once more, I marveled at the positive changes – it is now a beautiful and family friendly place.

But let me take you back 30 years to those incredible days when I served as a police lieutenant in a place that is now only a memory, a memory that I will carry with me all my days, a memory that changed my life forever.

I can say that because I was one of the lucky ones – I survived Fort Apache.

Prologue

IT IS DARK, very dark, on Fox Street in the South Bronx. A shadowy figure slides along the dark line of burnt-out buildings. He pauses in a garbage-strewn doorway. After a moment, he furtively moves on. Without warning, almost without sound, an arrow hurtles through the air. It makes a deep, sickening thud as it strikes the man. He crumples to the pavement. Several moments go by. The archer, George Washington Jones, creeps down the block, kneels, and examines his victim. He pulls out a knife and slashes the body with quick, savage strokes. When he turns to flee, he carries not only the bow but a crimson head of hair.

Later that night, Lieutenant Nat Clitter, desk officer of the Forty-first Precinct and a thirty-year veteran of the force, sits shaking his head. "I thought everything was possible in this place, and now I'm sure of it." On his desk lies the bow and the crimson head of hair.

He ignores the rookie who comes running into the room yelling, "Lieutenant, we're under attack." Jones's relatives and friends were coming to his aid.

Clitter looks up and smiles. "You'll get used to it," he says. Just then the telephone operator hollers for Clitter to pick up his phone. At the same time the first brick smashes against the iron grill outside a ground floor window. Clitter reels off several now-familiar orders: "Get the Polack inside and help him barri-cade the doors; turn off light switches one through four, thirteen and fourteen; and take your defensive positions."

A second brick passes through the grill, shatters the pane, and sends splintered glass cascading over the muster room floor. "Hello, hello," a voice yells in-credulously over the phone Clitter still holds in his hand. By now men in blue uniforms have slammed the huge front doors shut and are crouched around the windows. More bricks rain down against the ancient building.

"Ray," Clitter calls to his jail attendant, "Call a 10-13 [assist patrolman] on the station house." He still clutches the phone in his hand.

In all the confusion a dim voice can be heard cry-ing plaintively, "Hello, hello." Clitter ignores it. There are more important things to be done.

The lieutenant screams at an officer called Lotto: "You and the other guys with the baseball bats hit them first. If you see any knives or guns, fall back, and we'll fire a volley over their heads."

No one asks the almost unthinkable question: "And then what?"

An officer named Phil is told to get a shotgun out of the arms locker and hit the roof to cover any cars responding, to the scene. Lotto tells his baseball-bat squad, almost as if he were giving a pep talk to a soft-ball team, "Don't be fuckin' headhunters. Go for their ankles and knees."

"Another peaceful evening in the South Bronx," the Polack says. He has been watching the lieutenant in action. "That black bastard," he says, "is the best guy I ever worked for. He's got balls."

In the distance the sirens of responding units wail angrily through the hot night. Outside several attackers break through the barricaded door. With a sharp snap the door bursts open. "Bats!" the lieutenant shouts, and the five officers charge from their cover, swinging, and push the attackers back into the street. Lotto stands there, questioning their ancestry. Suddenly he hears several cracks and sees the flash of a rifle on the roof of a building across from the precinct. This seems to inject new confidence into the mob; it storms by the bat patrol and into the muster room waving knives, chains, and clubs.

Several officers in the rear fire a volley over the heads of the crowd. In the confusion, Lotto and his men have time to retreat. The second volley forces the rest of the group back into the street. One of the mob's inciters, a black named Oscar Brown and a friend of the arrested man, is cut down by a bat as he charges Lotto with a chain. By then, the field units have arrived and split the attackers into several containable groups. The voice on the phone is now yelling, "This is the Commissioner's Office. What the hell is going on there?" Clitter looks at the squeaking receiver as if he could break it in two.

"What the hell do you *think* is going on?" he screams. "This is Fort Apache." And he hangs up.

The muster room breaks up. "Fort Apache, Fort Apache," they yell to one another, laughing. "Fort Apache, that's it." The name sticks.

Outside, the battle swirls with small skirmishes fought up and down the street for another twenty minutes. Like so many similar battles that have been fought for so many years in the Four-one, there are neither winners nor losers, only victims. The people, mostly black, were angered because the Four-one had arrested another black man for killing a junkie. Guilty or innocent, it seemed so senseless. And later that day, George Washington Jones was arraigned for the murder of a junkie who had stolen a crimson wig from his wife.

1

MY NAME IS Tom Walker. I'm a hacker. If you've ever played schoolyard basketball, I was the type of guy with limited ability who tried to win the best way he could: with elbows, hands, almost anything available. So my rise in the force had been dogged, although not altogether brilliant.

After fourteen years in the Department, I had reached a long, sought-after plateau: lieutenant. I got my new assignment at the Police Academy Gymnasium on East 20th Street. A captain called off our commands: "Lieutenant Rosenthal, Manhattan South; Lieutenant Moss, Police Academy; Lieutenant Walker, Eighth Division . . ." I smiled, looked around, and found everyone else grinning. A rookie lieutenant going to the Eighth Division meant only one thing: the Four-one. My smile faded.

There was a mixture of emotions at my promotion party. My wife, Mary, was openly proud of my promotion, but quietly apprehensive about my assignment. My own pride had deeper roots: I was a fourth generation New York City cop. My great-grandfather was on the force during the Civil War Riots of 1863. My grandfather served during the first decade of this century. And my father put in nineteen years until an incident, involving charges that later proved untrue, forced him into retirement. My only regret was that he wasn't around to help me celebrate this day.

Mary wanted to know about the Four-one. I told her I thought stories other cops swapped about the place were overstated. Actually, I was a bit concerned. I'd been married fifteen years and had five beautiful children. The split shifts I'd work as a lieutenant would make me less available to my family. And deep in my gut I knew the Four-one would be no picnic.

At the time I went to the Four-one, I lived out of the city. Mary and I had been brought up in the Bronx, but had been lured away by a subtle combination of fear for our family's safety, prospective suburban tranquillity, and the peace of mind that comes with a twenty-year mortgage.

It was the spring of 1971 when I reported for my first night of duty at the Four-one. But driving south toward the city along the Palisades Parkway, I was oblivious to the blossoming shrubbery. Already I thought I knew a lot about the Four-one. Unofficially, the precinct had long been considered a dumping ground for fallen policemen and an ordeal by fire for rookies. What I eventually discovered was that the Four-one never shaped a man up the way the Department wanted it to. In some instances, duty at the precinct only increased the velocity of a man's slide to the bottom. On the other hand, it nurtured other qualities, such as courage and compassion, that might not have been fostered by other assignments.

Men assigned to the Four-one quickly became exiles. They were mavericks, loners, men who learned early on that to survive they had to absorb a set of values not taught in any training manual or in any course at the Police Academy. They sensed they were being punished and, like most men, they fought back with improvisation and, often, a desperate kind of humor. I suppose, and this may seem strange for an officer to say, they were asserting their individuality, something which both the Department and the precinct they patrolled denied them.

The Department has never fully understood what the Four-one does to a man, and the men knew this. It was this knowledge that drew them closer together. Their isolation gave them a special identity and sense of pride. That, I learned, was why the men in the muster room had laughed when Lieutenant Clitter called the precinct "Fort Apache." They were outcasts at the last outpost.

I'll admit to some misgivings that evening as I switched lanes and went across the George Washington Bridge. "Get out, Tom," a friend had advised me. "Get out as fast as you can. The Department is going to clean house and the Four-one will be hit especially hard." Another friend told me, "Promotion ends at the Four-one." A third added earnestly, "It's the Department's purgatory." I pressed down a bit harder on the gas.

I slipped off the expressway at Westchester Avenue and drove toward Simpson Street. The air felt much closer now and I could hear the animated speech of the stoop dwellers. Cars moved about seemingly without purpose, their inhabitants flipping empty beer cans into the street. Then the driver would punch the accelerator and the car would screech off, oblivious to anyone in its path.

The Four-one is quartered in a Neo-Florentine building. It was built around the turn of the century with a square, flat roof. Each window is framed at the top by a graceful arch. When I drew up to the curb I could see only the ugly concrete slabs covered with grime. I knew it was a police station because there were bars on the windows and behind the windows were thick, steel shields.

Protocol dictates that a lieutenant has a parking space reserved for him in front of the house. When I drove up, all the slots were taken. So I parked around the corner on Fox Street. Then I hoofed it back to the station house.

New sensations assaulted me. The air was filled with strange odors that I would come to identify as cuchifritos and planta, all part of the multitude of dishes that, when spread over a plate of steaming rice, constitutes the indigenous diet. A large part of the Four-one's inhabitants are classified as Puerto Ricans. Actually, Puerto Ricans constitute the majority of the Spanish-speaking population, but there are also Dominicans, Cubans, and a few Venezuelans. In time, I would realize the subtle differences.

As I walked down Fox Street, my shoes made a crunching sound that reminded me of walking along a beach, but the "sand" was finely ground glass, stretching from one curb to the other. Small children played boisterous tag along the sidewalks; clusters of men sipped beer on the stoops. Burned-out buildings cast eerie shadows across my path. Automobiles slumped like derelicts, abandoned, stripped of their former dignity and supported only by milk cases. The street itself was full of holes, a pockmarked face on the verge of total degeneration.

At the end of the block, a gang harassed an elderly couple with whistles and obscenities as the pair skirted the edge of a playground, also covered with shards of glass. The playground equipment, the slides, the basketball backboard all yawed at awkward angles, broken and neglected.

On Simpson Street, the only area with any adequate lighting and without a mound of rotting garbage in front of it, was the precinct house. As I approached on foot, the building seemed even sterner and more forbidding in the darkness, less a refuge than a fortress. But then all those dark tenements were fortresses of a sort, depending for their safety on the strength of their inhabitants and the abilities of the men in the precinct. In that sense, the station house was a part of the neighborhood. And yet it was separate. As an institution, some residents looked to it for aid; others saw it as a target for their scorn, even rage.

There was a single patrolman on duty as I approached the entrance. He was talking to two shabbily dressed men whose unshaven faces were picked out by the harsh light. I decided to ignore their excited voices and headed for the door.

Suddenly the patrolman was jolted off his feet and fell against me. We crashed backward into the vestibule. The shouting increased in volume and I realized that the side of my shirt was wet and sticky with his blood. As I lay sprawled on the floor, I noticed that my attaché case had broken open, spreading papers across the floor, including my copy of *Playboy*.

One of the two men I had seen outside came rushing through the doorway, swinging an iron pipe. Behind him came the second man carrying a knife. I'm big and not that quick, but I moved fast this time. As the guy with the knife rushed past his friend, I met him with a right to the gut. He folded like a sack of laundry and rolled back out onto the sidewalk. The patrolman recovered quickly and jumped the other man who had the pipe. The guy I had hit turned and ran down the street. I pulled out my revolver and started to pursue, but it was no-contest. He was well away. When I stopped running, I found that my hand was shaking uncontrollably.

By the time I returned to the station house, the man with the pipe had been subdued. I was covered with blood and still breathing hard. I had hoped to make a dignified entry on my first tour, but instead I dragged my tail in looking more like a victim than a victor. Gathering up my papers and *Playboy* along with my pride, I went into the muster room of the Four-one.

Dirty and dimly lit, like an enormous cavern filled with mysterious, dark corners and with numerous dank passages leading away from it, the muster room was almost an extension of the neighborhood itself. Dust and paint particles fell from the ceiling.

The room, filled with busy officers and anxious civilians, was humming. Near the door, to my left, a large busty woman sat interviewing another woman who held a crying child. As I walked by her desk, she stood up and lifted her knit blouse, revealing a pair of enormous, well-supported breasts. "Hey," she yelled. "You like? Better than *Playboy*, huh?"

I couldn't believe it and I guess my amazement showed. The men in the muster room broke into laughter. What the hell have I gotten myself into? I asked myself. I soon learned that I had just endured one of the Four-one's more obvious forms of hazing. Rosa, one of our helpful civilian receptionists, had given me her ritual greeting.

The laughter quickly dissipated when groans were heard from the rear of the room. The patrolman who had been attacked with the pipe had received a serious head injury. A couple of officers picked him up and carried him to a patrol car. The car, with siren blasting, headed for Lincoln Hospital.

Some patrolmen came in to ask about the wounded officer, whose name was Grant. The situation was pretty tense, so I identified myself and told the men to cool down. I ordered the men back on patrol and, within an hour, Patrolman Grant returned with sixteen stitches in his head.

"The bastards picked a lousy night to fool with a cop," said the desk sergeant.

"What do you mean?" I asked.

"You didn't hear?" he said, and went on to tell me about the killing of two cops in the Three-two.

"They were ambushed in the Polo Grounds' housing project in Harlem, near 155th Street. The BLA or some shit like that. Nine or ten shots at close range. Christ, when I think of the scum walking around out there! And these guys have to get it for no goddamn reason except that they're cops. Shit!"

It shouldn't be hard to explain the reaction one cop has to another cop's death. But it is. In the back of your mind you always know it might have been you. And, in addition to defending himself, a cop also has to be able to publicly justify every move he makes in the process. Never mind who hurled the first word or tossed the first stone or held the shotgun. A cop *must* always be in the right. So people are slow to mourn a fallen officer and we must bear our grief largely in silence.

"What were their names?" I asked.

"Here, it was on the teletype. Joseph Piagintini and Waverly Jones.

The face came back to me. A handsome, smiling, evenly chiseled black face. Waverly Jones. We had worked together in the 46th Precinct on patrol. I really didn't know him that well. We had coffee a few times together and I remember him as a real decent guy. I had known him for a short time; then we had gone our own ways. Now he was dead. I would like to think that I was stunned more for the loss of the man than for the loss of a fellow cop. I quickly asked where the locker room was.

It was in the basement; more correctly, it should have been called a swamp. To reach my locker, I had to wade through half a foot of putrid, mosquito-infested water. Raw sewage poured into the room and several large, menacing rodents sought neutral corners only when I began to growl at them. This was enough. Across from the locker room, a door had a sign above it that read Lunch Room. Appalled, I went back upstairs. The commanding officer (C.O.) of the Four-one was a captain. His office was empty and Savage, the desk sergeant, told me that the captain generally wasn't in after six. I was also told that the patrolmen were encouraged to use the basement; it helped them to better understand the neighborhood.

I closed the door, sat down at the desk, and contemplated the Four-one. A patrolman knocked on the door. He went over to the captain's closet and pulled out a bottle of Johnny Walker Red. "The sergeant wanted to know if you'd like a short one, Lou," he said. I nodded. I would have to get used to being called Lou, a shortened version of lieutenant used throughout the Department. It took a week before I responded to someone yelling, "Hey, Lou."

After he left, I gulped down the shot and felt better. As he poured the shot, the patrolman had remarked that it looked as if the captain was expecting me. Sitting there, I realized why he sensed I would need the booze to get me over those first rough minutes. I still had doubts about the precinct and myself, but I knew that somehow it all had to be turned around.

The captain had also anticipated some questions. Normal questions such as, "Where the hell am I? I found a folder on his desk, addressed to me. It contained basic facts. Population: 171,000–92,000 Puerto Ricans, 73,000 blacks, and 6,000 designated as others. To cover this area the captain had 336 patrolmen, no policewomen, 22 sergeants, and 4 lieutenants. The precinct had a detective squad with a reputation for getting quick results. The Four-one was 2.5 square miles in area with 60 miles of streets. It was divided into seventeen sectors that were identified by letter. A radio motor patrol (RMP) car was assigned to police each sector. Each sergeant on a given tour was assigned a number of sectors to supervise. Lieutenants, at that time, were utilized only for desk duty. Army terminology was used for radio purposes. The dispatcher, holding a job in Sector E, would call, "Sector Eddie," give the location, frequently omitting the words "street" or "avenue," and then give the nature of the job in concise terms. A typical call in the Four-one might be, "Sector Eddie, Fox and Kelly, man shot." Air time had to be minimized to handle the workload.

I plowed through the list of known gamblers and their associates. There were also lists of social relig-ious, and governmental organizations. I noted that

45,000 people in the area were on welfare. In the back of the file were listed identifiable youth gangs that were then a growing but unpublicized trend among youngsters. Somehow, though, I sensed that I had not seen the essence of the Four-one. This knowledge, I knew, would not come until I hit the streets.

As I sat there, I also perused the personnel folders of the men.

Captain Ryan's folder had been stripped. He apparently had anticipated someone like me thumbing through it. Typical, I thought to myself. His reputation was that of a tart, tough, and smart boss.

I found Sergeant Bartow's interesting. He had served in the toughest precincts in Manhattan, the 9th, 28th, and 32nd. He's seen it all, I mused. He had been shot once. He had received one complaint but had about fifteen medals for outstanding work. I would find out later that it was the complaint that got him to the Four-one. His record was impressive; I looked forward to meeting him.

As I flipped through the folders I noticed that one officer had worked in the Four-seven when my father was there. I made a mental note to speak to him later about Dad.

A scream from the muster room brought me to my feet. A head appeared at the door, "It's okay, only a prisoner," the officer said.

I went back to the folders. Sergeant Savage had a poor record. Disciplinary transfers from one precinct to another. They had run out of places to send him; anything after the Four-one would be a step upward.

I continued to flip the manila folders: A Patrolmen Ruth. Ruth was a college graduate with an excellent

14

record; a comer, I thought. Another mental note, look for him.

From my quick inspection, I figured that 75 percent of the men had been in the Four-one for several years or more. The others were either disciplinary transfers or rookies.

When I relieved Savage at the desk, he asked me if I had learned anything yet.

"Yeah," I growled. "You can't wear pants with cuffs around here," shaking a pair of cockroaches loose.

He laughed and then we got down to business. He showed me how to sound the alarm that would alert men in the station house that an emergency situation had arisen. Then he showed me how the log was kept, how the phones were set up, and what numbers were used frequently. It was all pretty routine.

As he got up to leave, his face took on a harder edge. "It's been bad here lately, or I should say worse," he said. "They arrested two of the guys last night on a drug rap. Bad news. And the men think it was setup. Who knows?" He picked up some papers. "But with those arrests, the guys shot in the Three-two, what happened to Grant tonight, crap, you name it. You can't blame a lot of the guys if they get the feeling that it's them against the world."

I had no answer. I hadn't realized that the morale in the Four-one had reached such a low level. "Don't worry Lou," Savage said, "you'll probably get to know it all before the night is over." He was right. That night, although I had seventeen cars on the street, I could have used forty.

From the first, the desk radio seemed like an insane, antiquated Victrola, playing the same squawking tunes. "Four-one David. Respond to Seneca and Long-fellow. Disorderly group on the street . . ." And so it went. All night the anger and the violence and the gore poured electronically across my desk. It must have been hell out there, because I only saw the bitter remnants – refugees would be a better word – the ones they brought in.

First, the Tactical Patrol Force (TPF) brought in four kids for burglary, a felony. I knocked it down to criminal trespass, a misdemeanor. You have to call them as you see them. Finally they left, grumbling over their lost felony arrests. A woman walked in with her entire family and in-laws. The complaint: that afternoon the woman's daughter was married; that night, the groom locked the bride out of the apartment. My sergeant, Carl Bartow, and I laughed slightly and he offered to take a ride over to the apartment.

Then Sector Adam came bouncing through the door leading a man who wore only a large grin. A prostitute had robbed the guy and taken his clothes so he wouldn't give chase. He did anyway. "We saw him running down Southern Boulevard," one of the patrolmen said. "We knew something was up when we realized he wasn't jogging." The man was good-natured about the whole affair and we tried to round up some clothes for him.

Our laughter subsided when another man stumbled into the station house covered with blood. His clothes had been sliced to shreds. This is one of the common types of serious crime in the Four-one. Usually two or more people will jump the victim. They want to act fast, so they rip his pockets with razor blades, grabbing whatever valuables fall out. It's inefficient but pretty frightening. Often, the assailants get carried away and stab or stomp their victim, which accounted for this man's blood.

As he told the story, he saw the other guy standing stark naked in the corner. He started laughing. Perhaps it was sympathetic laughter. Perhaps he was happy to see someone in almost as miserable shape as himself. We couldn't help but join in. A gallows sense of humor helped a lot in the Four-one.

Since work was piling up, I sent Sergeant Bartow over to check up on the newlyweds. I had quickly realized that there is no way to anticipate some of the problems that will arise in this precinct.

An attendant, sweeping behind the desk, asked me if I played "running chess." I admitted that I played chess, but that I didn't know what running chess was. It turned out that the kid was a real freak on the game and that he had a game going with everyone in the house. He had chess-boards at five different locations. As he made his rounds, he made his moves.

Sergeant Bartow came back to file his report and moved to a magnetic chessboard near the side door. He noticed me watching and said with admirable chess logic, "White has had it now. Black has moved from the defensive to the offensive and now has superior position. I can't wait to capture the white queen." I looked at the board and realized he was a better than average player.

"Speaking of kings and queens," I said, "how are our honeymooners doing?"

"She married some kind of astrology nut, or so he claims. Says it would be fatal for him to give himself at this time. We nearly had a fight when one of the drunks in the bridal party offered to give of himself instead. What a crew. The mother finally took the bride home."

Several minutes later, Sergeant Ted Grit, police novel in hand, strolled into the house, just as Bartow was leaving. Bartow laughed. "Ted, why are you reading that trash? Tomorrow I'll bring you a real good book to read."

"What's it called?"

"The Black Knight." Besides being bright and physically handsome, Bartow was also black. He started to whistle as he went through the door.

The jobs kept rolling in, and that's what they were, just jobs. Even the names had little significance. I spent eight hours booking thirty-four prisoners, arguing with or offering advice to an equal number of people, making decisions, making notifications, directing the men in the station house and, while I was at it, consuming what must have been an urn of coffee. The patrolman on security in front of the station house was a great help, acting as a buffer and letting no one inside who didn't have a real problem. After two years away from a desk, I needed all the help I could get. By sunrise, all that standing and leaning over my desk left me exhausted. Meals and coffee breaks are not guaranteed by a union contract. If you're busy, you eat as you work. My back ached and it seemed like the tour would never end. I wondered how long I could take this pace.

As I walked toward my car in the early morning light, the area didn't seem quite so threatening. The street was vacant now, the doorways empty, the windows dark and silent. It was as if hate and violence were napping. The garbage was there, but I couldn't attach people to it, or it to people. Alleys leaned above me, sharp and clean as canyons.

When I hit Fox Street I stopped. There sat my car – on four milk boxes. I had nothing left. I felt no emotion. A patrol car stopped. "Hi, Lou," one of the men said. "Need a lift?"

I forced a smile. "You haven't seen four Sears Special tires anywhere, have you?"

From that day on, I made sure that I parked right in front of the station house. Unfortunately everyone couldn't park there and daily incidents occurred; batteries stolen, cars stolen, windows broken, tires stolen, aerials broken off, the list goes on. Once, a Patrolman Huff was going up the Taconic Parkway when his left rear wheel fell off. He was lucky to escape with his life. A check of the other tires revealed that the lug nuts had been loosened on all of them. I was slowly learning that all the attacks on us were directed at our uniforms and not to our persons.

It seemed that the precinct was loaded with scavengers. Anyone caught stripping a car in the vicinity of the station house was shown no mercy. Waiting for my new tires to arrive, I thought about an executive problem-solving exercise that I had taken in the Police Academy. The problem was a real one that confronted authorities in Atlanta, Georgia. What fascinated me was that the Atlanta Social Welfare Department opposed a police department plan to remove vehicles without plates from the streets within forty-eight hours. That department claimed that stripping cars and selling the parts was an important source of income in the section of town known as Vine City. It helped supplement welfare payments. They claimed it took a car stripper at least a week to find a buyer, get the part, and deliver it. As a result, they recommended that the police rule be extended to seven days. I can't speak for the Vine section of Atlanta, but many of the cars stolen in New York City are taken to Fort Apache and then stripped for parts. Most parts are sold. It's big business. It seems ludicrous not to remove these vehicles as soon as possible. I idly wondered how much of my car would be left after seven days.

It cost me a hundred dollars and two hours sleep before the car was ready to roll again. I drove straight home. My wife sensed that something was wrong, but she didn't press me. She knew that eventually I would tell her the whole story. Exhausted, I went to bed.

2

ON MONDAY MORNING I met the commanding officer, Captain Nick Ryan. He was a short, good-looking Irishman with a sharp nose and a trim crew cut. He projected the image of a Marine drill sergeant, and I later realized that that was precisely the image he wanted to present. He didn't talk much, but when he said something, nobody questioned it – except me. If I smiled, he would say, "Tom, there's nothing to smile about in this place. I suggest you get your ass on patrol." I'm sure this is the way he talked to his patrolmen when he was a sergeant. He had only recently been assigned here and was promptly greeted by the arrest of several of his men by the Internal Affairs Division of the Police Department. Two had been arrested for possession of drugs, one for shaking down practically anyone he came across, and a couple of officers arrested for trying to shake down a junkyard/stolen car ring. I don't believe he thought it possible, but as he began to accomplish things, he developed an affection for the men and the place. He too began to delight in our mutual misery.

We sat and discussed the precinct's problems. In that quiet office, we spoke of thousands of rapes, robberies, and assaults. He told me the projected number of homicides for the year was well over 100. Actually, the total is open to debate. I counted 137, but some might have been reclassified as suicides. A detective quoted me 112 and *The New York Times* claimed 102. Even this latter figure puts the number of murders in this small dark area ahead of such cities as Kansas City, Miami, and San Francisco. Ryan said that the number of calls for service would probably hit 100,000 before the year was over. This seemed incredible, but it turned out the Four-one did respond to more radio runs than any other precinct in the city and probably in the country.

Of course we also make more arrests than any other precinct in the city. More crime, more arrests. The lower the ship sank, the more water it took in. In any event, we wound up working our butts off. I've never been sure of the solution. At sometime, I'm sure, the criminal has to be reached and rehabilitated. We can't keep arresting people and throwing them in jail only to see them reemerge criminally smarter but with more hatred, defiant, and resigned to a desperate future. All I was sure of were the facts, depressing facts, such as the one that nine out of ten people who die on Fox Street do so as a result of unnatural causes (drugs, homicide, suicide, rats, lead poisoning, etc.). Statistics, though, will never adequately measure the suffering of people. There is no breakdown for suffering and misery on a computer printout.

At this meeting, Capt. Ryan told me I was going back to the street. In 1971, Howard Leary was out and Patrick Murphy was in as Police Commissioner. Murphy shook up much of the complacency that had been so prevalent in the Department. He was active and attentive to detail. Above all, he had a keen mind and a penchant for innovation.

One of his ideas was the Operations Officer concept or O/O as it became known. The Four-one was one of the first precincts where O/O was introduced. Essentially, the idea is to put the lieutenant into the field and replace him with a station house supervisor (usually a sergeant) and a station house officer (usually a patrolman). This operation did not lessen the lieutenant's responsibilities. In fact, he had more to do since he was not only playing a more active role in street operations but was also held responsible for the efficient operation of the station house. This program had the effect of enlarging and enriching the lieutenant's job. He was encouraged to be aggressive and innovative. Captain Ryan kept telling me, "For chrissake, Tom, make some moves. You keep telling me what's wrong. Here's a chance to do something about it."

At the same time, the O/O concept also reduced, in practice, the number of supervisors reporting directly to the C.O. Under the old system, if the C.O. wanted to know something about field conditions, he had to consult with one or several of over twenty sergeants. Now he had only to talk with one of four lieutenants. It made things a lot simpler and, I felt, helped bring the lieutenant further into the total picture. I thought the program was a sound idea.

As I moved around the station house checking records, I noticed an elderly man also walking around talking to the men. Someone told me he was Sid Broun, a German Jew who had lived in the precinct for many years. He was a retired postal worker who had been a close friend of Mayor William O'Dwyer. Twice a week he came in to B.S. for a couple of hours, discussing the rumors he had picked up downtown. He still had friends at headquarters and was always trying to help someone get out of the precinct.

One of the clerical men suggested that if I wanted a history lesson of the precinct, I should take Sid with me when I toured the area. I introduced myself and he agreed to come along. It was the beginning of a lasting friendship.

As we drove, he talked about the neighborhood. "My family came to Fox Street about 1901," he recalled. "It was the country in those days. My relatives from Manhattan would spend a couple of weeks with us in the summer. It was Tom Sawyer time on Fox Street. Would you believe it? They should see it now.

"Back then, the neighborhood took great pride in everything, especially its gardens and orchards. We had a cherry tree in our backyard. It died years back because of all the pollution.

"Everybody shared their fruit in those days. There were outhouses; we burned coal for heat and for cooking. There were no street lights and, most importantly, there were no criminals. The streets in the area still carry the names of those people." As we drove, he ticked them off. Fox, Simpson, Tiffany, Vyse, Chisholm, all had housed great estates once. Now their spacious lawns were broad reaches of asphalt and the houses were crumbling like frail cinders.

He talked of the fine mansions along Prospect Avenue and then described the first elevator apartment. Moe DeVito, the officer I had picked as my steady driver, suddenly laughed. "They must have stopped after the first one," he said. "Because to my knowledge," he added, "there's only one building in this precinct with an elevator shaft, much less an elevator."

Sid didn't argue the point. Instead he told us about the building of the subway up Westchester Avenue and how he had watched Morris High School being built from his "secret place" in the attic of his house. He was at the opening of the Four-one in 1914, although he believed it had a different numerical designation then.

As we passed the area where a Colonel Hoe's house had stood, he talked about his first wife, Jane, a relative of the colonel. "Yes," he said, "God was here in those days. Now it seems like God got off Fox Street."

I changed the subject and suggested we go to Joe's on Hunts Point Avenue for some coffee and danish. Sid smiled knowingly. He added as an afterthought; "You know, Tom, if you look closely you can still see some relics from the past here." It was my turn to smile.

Later, after dropping Sid off at the corner of Fox and Prospect, I was glad I hadn't made any comments about the present-day squalor that pervaded the precinct. After all, it was still his home. But from what I had seen, the city had written off these people as though they were used clothes or unredeemable lottery tickets.

The only vestige of civilized authority here was the Police Department. The people struck me as being rather primitive in their approach to city life. Many seemed to be travelers in a strange world. Urbanization would wait for the next generation. They didn't hesitate to throw garbage into the streets, or drive without a license, or take the law into their own hands. Without any regard for the rights of others, they did what they wanted. Part of it, I suppose, was the culture that demanded that a man, to be a man, must always save face. This concept of *machismo* compelled a man to react with violence to any threatening situation.

As I reentered the station house, the captain asked me about my tour. "I don't think I've seen anything worse," I remember saying. He smiled. I didn't realize it then, but that was the most peaceful day I was to spend in the Four-one.

3

THE DESK SERGEANT that night was a man named Alexis. As he pressed the buzzer that summoned the men to roll call, I skimmed the assignment sheet to see if there had been any changes. Moe waved as he walked into the sitting room. In the rear of the station house, on the first floor, was the sitting room. Here roll call and training were conducted before each tour. It was a typical Friday night. The station house seemed almost happy as the men flooded into the muster room after roll call, talking and laughing. Ahead of them was the street. They would hit it on foot or in patrol cars. And without their partners, they would have been very much alone.

The previous night, Moe and I had spent our first full tour together. It had been a smooth one. You quickly learn, if you're going to last on the force, that the key to getting along on patrol is small talk. All right, disagree on major issues, but if you can't make small talk, you'll never last as partners. That's the way you have to think all the time – that you and the guy next to you are partners; the most important thing is to protect each other. When you do that, you protect yourself. The boss, the man with superior rank or seniority, may give the orders, but only a fool would forget the nights he got home safely because his partner was where he was supposed to be, doing what he was supposed to do.

It's all a part of what it feels like to be a cop. To the people on the street, you and your partner are just two bodies in two blue uniforms. It makes no difference that I'm a lieutenant and Moe is a patrolman. As one black cop told me, "Up here, in uniform, even if you're white, it's like being black. No matter how high you go, you're still identified by your generic name." A cop is a cop is a cop, I remember thinking to myself after that remark. So I was pleased that things seemed to be working out well between Moe and myself.

The patrol supervisor, Sergeant Saverin, told me that a man was needed to guard a psychologically disturbed prisoner at Lincoln Hospital; another man had to stand watch over a DOA on Kelly Street. It meant losing a car, but it was the only solution. Procedure, after all, is procedure.

With a DOA, or, more explicitly, a body, "dead on arrival," even if the death is not the direct result of a crime, the police usually have to inventory whatever property exists on the premises and report the death to the medical examiner (M.E.) Then a patrolman is assigned to the area until the M.E. arrives, looks at the body, and signs a release. Then someone has to be there to get a receipt from an undertaker or an ambulance attendant.

A psychologically disturbed person is another problem. A patrolman is needed to wait in a hospital receiving unit in case the man or woman should try to escape or attack someone. It isn't the best duty available. At least a corpse won't fight you.

The sergeant was trying to locate the most unproductive pair of men when a Patrolman Sock volunteered for the DOA. Sock was indeed unproductive; he didn't issue many summonses or make arrests, but more importantly, he didn't handle his share of radio runs. His request was still a little unusual. While the assignment wasn't particularly demanding, many of the men thought it undesirable. Policemen, like a lot of workers, don't enjoy disruptions in their routine, particularly when such disruptions are caused by distasteful chores. Maybe Sock knew something, I reasoned. A DOA is better than a psycho and, by volunteering, his partner would get the pleasure of sitting with the psycho, whether he liked it or not.

The roll had been called and the outgoing platoon inspected before I made my way to the sitting room. I could hear Saverin's voice loud and clear: "Let's pick up the phone, you guys. The captain's getting on my ass about those radio backlogs; if it don't start to get any better, I'm going to start breaking them." A radio backlog is when the dispatcher is holding jobs and there are no cars available to take them. It was a growing problem in the Four-one.

He went on, "Remember, on these crowded streets, we go in and do what we have to do and we get out. Don't get involved in any shouting matches. Make your arrest, whatever, and leave. The longer we stay, the greater the chance for problems. Watch your ass out there. Don't wander off and leave your partner for too long. Remember what happened to Harris."

Later Saverin filled me in on Harris. Harris and his partner had been chasing the junkies off their post. One night his partner wandered off, leaving Harris alone. The junkies jumped Harris, beating him seriously.

I went over and stood beside the sergeant and he asked me if I had anything to say. A short speech on community relations floated at the back of my mind, but it seemed inappropriate. What the hell, I had seen the Four-one. Was I going to convince men who faced, every day, the worst murderers, thieves, and rapists in the city, that by doing their duty they wouldn't face, the very next day, the same murderers, thieves, and rapists? It wouldn't work and I knew it. So I grabbed for some formula speech from the Police Academy, the kind of pep talk the Police Commissioner usually gives rookies.

"Gentlemen," I said, and immediately realized how pompous I sounded. But I plunged ahead: "Please make sure that your T-shirts are not showing." I couldn't begin to guess how many of the men suppressed a laugh when they heard that beautiful opening statement.

"I have also noticed some officers with their hats off while outside their patrol car. I don't think this is the type of image we want to develop." I pointed to one man standing in the first rank and said, "Officer Scanlon, before you leave the station house, polish those shoes."

Then, unable to think of anything equally silly to add, I turned to the sergeant and told him to post the platoon. As the men left the muster room, I could sense them thinking almost as one "Is this guy for real?" I knew I had blown my first impression and resolved to learn how to think faster on my feet.

Still feeling chagrined, I faced my most immediate problem. The sergeant had been directed to visit a social club on Bristow Street and find out if any violations were being committed there. Usually these violations meant selling liquor without a license, or gambling. In some cases there was a suspicion of prostitution.

Since this was a Friday night and since the social club was popular with many local residents, the sergeant suggested that it might be hazardous to take any immediate action. To my regret, I took a rather rigid stand. "If that's what the C.O. wants," I told him, "that's what we'll do." The sergeant looked annoyed as he turned away. Moe was waiting as I slid into the radio car.

We coasted to the Hunts Point diner and picked up two containers of coffee. Then we headed for the end of Hunts Point Avenue. There the warehouses were dark and very few people walked the streets. We sat and sipped the coffee and watched the planes descend gracefully toward La Guardia Airport across Long Island Sound. The radio was quiet and we were in a talkative mood.

During his time in the armed forces, Moe had been a flyer with a squadron of hurricane hunters stationed in Jacksonville, Florida. He also reminisced about the time he served with the Neptunes, a sub-hunting group that flew out of Floyd Bennett Field in Brooklyn. It was ironic that we were thrown together like this because one of my many unrealized ambitions was to become a pilot. I told Moe how I lost my nerve.

I had been a rookie at the time and they were tying to teach me how to chase speeders. One day, in desperate pursuit, with the speedometer at 75 m.p.h., the kingpin of my '55 Ford snapped and the car flipped over. It was messy. I remember vividly the concerned face of Freddy Watts, one of the first to reach the scene, as he placed his police jacket under my head. Another officer, Tom Lamont, cracked jokes. I didn't have the strength to laugh. The one person's name I can't remember was a former army medic who applied pressure at the right points and helped stem the bleeding.

Honorary Police Surgeon Black sliced me up and stitched me back together in an operation that lasted over five hours. Over two hundred stitches helped close the wound in my head. After that, I learned to love planes from the ground.

Moe's response to the story was typical. "Are you sure they stitched everything back in place?" he mocked.

For a moment I was startled, then I found myself laughing. "If you want," I said, "I'll get an affidavit from my wife. And believe me, she feels overworked as it is."

Moe grinned. "Braggart," he said.

The radio began to chatter. We moved toward the center of the precinct. That move meant we would be in a position to back up any unit in almost any direction. As we drove up Hunts Point Avenue, we noticed Sector David talking to a man in a '71 Oldsmobile. Moe read off the plate number. "It's a habit," he said. "In case anything happens, I have a plate number."

Later we discovered that the car belonged to Harry Williams. He owned an ice cream business in Westchester and had apparently done quite well. Part of his success was due to the way he treated his employees. He felt the loyalty of his twenty drivers was unquestionable and that such loyalty deserved reward.

That Friday he decided to visit a sick driver in Lincoln Hospital. Unfamiliar with the Bronx, he became lost and stopped Sector David to ask for directions. That was when we passed by.

Seconds later, directions fresh in his head, he turned up Fox Street. Perhaps because he wasn't familiar with the unpredictable nature of the neighborhood or perhaps because his mind was preoccupied with his mission, Williams didn't see the dog that dashed out into the street. He slammed on his brakes, but it was too late. With a sharp yelp, the dog was hurled to the sidewalk, dead. Then Williams made his second mistake. He stopped.

Before he could get out of the car, an angry crowd gathered. First they broke the car's windows. Of course accidents of this kind happen every day on Fox Street, and without meaning to sound calloused, many of the residents consider the hundreds of stray animals in the area a nuisance. But Williams was an outsider. So when they were through with the windows, they pulled open the hood and methodically tore out engine parts.

Both terrified and angry, Williams got out of the car and tried to stop them. He heard two sudden cracks, like a whip snapping, and his legs buckled under him. A third bullet struck him in the side.

Unsatisfied, the crowd turned the car on its side and set it on fire. Then they argued about whether or not they should flip the burning car over on Williams. That was when Sector John arrived. The scene attracted more people and it became festive as the light from the burning fire painted the street a warm orange and the crowd laughed and chatted in apparent celebration.

By the time we got there, no one had quite sorted out the facts. Firemen arrived and immediately displayed their disgust. This was the second car fire alarm they had answered on this block that day. We took Williams to the hospital where he spent the night sharing the room of the employee he originally intended to visit.

Moe was still angry when we got back to the car. "They ought to be shot," he said.

"If we knew who was involved," I said., "we'd lock them up."

He laughed. "They'd be out tomorrow. Up here, they get three years for a homicide. The courts treat ghetto murders like a joke. Just stay here a while and you'll learn.

"Look, they send us sergeants and lieutenants who can't take the street. They stay a day, a week, a month, and then they get on the phone, making calls all over the place to get out of here. The average cop can't get out. Then they send some psychologist or sociologist up here to look the place over and he says we're defensive and have a bad attitude." He stared out the window and then started the engine. "Crap," he said under his breath as we headed for 149th Street.

We made the rounds and I signed the memo books of the patrolmen on beats. After a while Moe said, "That's it. I think we've covered them all."

I checked the sheet. "Wait a minute," I said. "What about the guy with the DOA?"

Something was wrong. "Look, Lou," Moe said. "The other sergeants and lieutenants usually didn't bother with the men on DOA's. Where are they going to go?"

I knew this wasn't the case. If anything, DOA's are treated very seriously. What he was really saying finally reached me. It's a tradition in the Department that if you are going to be off base, you tell the telephone switchboard (TS) operator and the boss's chauffeur to cover your tracks. That way, the TS operator covers you inside, the chauffeur outside. If someone in the station house is looking for you, the first person checked is the TS operator; he can then alert you that you're wanted. If the boss in the street wants you, his driver will know where you are. This was the first problem to develop since Moe began driving for me.

"We better straighten out signals," I said. "I don't expect you to rat on anyone, but there aren't any free rides, not anymore. I don't want any of this 'but I told it to your chauffeur' bullshit."

Moe nodded and pulled away from the curb. I could feel that things between us had suddenly tensed up. While I was concerned, I was also equally determined to see some sense of discipline restored to the Four-one. Moe said nothing as he swung the car toward Kelly Street.

Finally, I had to ask, "What's with this guy Sock?"

He shrugged his shoulders. "You'll find out soon enough.

The silence between us was almost as unbearable as the heat. Partnerships, I have come to realize, have the same permanence as paper towels. Depending upon circumstances, some hold up well for a while; others fall apart almost immediately. Both of us were very uneasy, and very quiet, all the way to the Kelly Street address.

I went in alone, although I wasn't sure what I would find. In one hand was a walkie-talkie and in the other my nightstick. The tenement was dark; the stairs shaky. I needed quiet. But while I paused on the third floor landing, the walkie-talkie cracked, "Sockie, Sockie." Moe warning Sock of my impending arrival. Why? For a moment anger ran through me. My first thought was to drop Moe as my driver.

When I knocked on the door, I could hear a lot of scuffling inside. I yelled for Moe and started kicking the door. Since I weigh around 275, the door gave way on the fourth try.

A pretty, young Puerto Rican girl jumped back as I burst through the door. The room was a mess – worn-out rugs, furniture that had probably been discarded by some bargain store. And in the middle of it all, a half-naked girl nosed among the debris for the rest of her clothes.

In the bedroom, Sock tried vainly to wriggle into his gunbelt. "Hi, Lou," he said with a grin. "Wanna drink?" Beside the bed lay a half-empty pint of rye.

I was at my officious best: "So that's what you do. Set up a phony DOA so you can party."

"Nah," he said and tried to sit down, but his legs were too shaky to get him to the nearest chair. "The DOA's legit. Just a guy who died with no relatives around. I just move it into the bathtub and cover it up." So while the body stiffened in the tub, Sock invited the girl up for a party. And he had done it before, I was sure.

The girl dressed quickly, almost professionally, but Moe prevented her from leaving. That was a plus in his favor. So far the count was two-and-one. Moe, as if sensing my dilemma, came up beside me. "Lou," he said, "the guy's a lush, an alkie. I don't know half his problems, and the half I know I would rather forget."

I was confronted with a problem that undoubtedly meant unraveling years of Sock's life. And I didn't have the time. The girl was crying, soft tears that poured easily and dried just as quickly. She would be no help so I sent her scurrying down the stairs. We took Sock back to the station house and told him to take the night off. I reported the situation to the C.O.

Several days later, Sock was transferred to the chaplain's office.

In the New York City Police Department, chaplains do more than appear for benedictions or funerals. One of the office's chief functions is to help men with drinking problems. Usually the men work in that section for a while; hopefully they make an effort at licking their problem. If they relapse or become worse, they are taken, sometimes under duress, to a farm in northern New Jersey where they are dried out. I suppose I should be shocked that a department dedicated to law enforcement can take action that comes close to kidnapping. But sometimes the guy is cured and his job saved. And at least the Department hasn't given up on a man although it can be pretty rough on him. What happened to Sock, I don't know. My depression lasted through that night.

Afterward, over sandwiches, Moe tried to explain. "This has been going on for a long time," he said. "Most of the bosses knew about it. You're new and you didn't. So why should you be any different and have to handle a problem others refused to face? Why didn't the other guys do it?"

He took a bite out of his sandwich, looked around, and then came back to me. "I'm your chauffeur. If you catch a guy real bad, you got to hurt him real bad. So for you and him, I try to do the right thing. That's why I called up there. He's really no good, a drunk, a lover, a fighter, but no cop. Still, he's got a family. See what I mean?"

He was temporizing and he knew that I knew it. One guy messing around, particularly in this precinct, meant one less guy in the streets or in a car, and I needed all the bodies I could get. But this was one body I didn't need. "Look, I know you were on the spot. But if I'm going to last more than a month here, I've got to know all the problems."

For a long moment we sat there. "Okay, no more bullshit," he said.

From that moment, Moe and I developed, an unshakable feeling of trust. Although he never broke the bonds he had with the men, he played it eye to eye with me. In light of a conversation I overheard several days later, his loyalty was all the more surprising.

I was calling Mary to find out if the date for the closing had been set. We were in the process of selling our home and moving back to the Bronx. We missed the excitement and the conveniences. As I picked up the phone, I heard no dial tone, just voices. Assuming the TS operator had left a button up, I searched for another line. What the voices said stopped me.

"You want me to check him, okay," one voice said. "But I'll have to ask for a squad change to get close to him."

"Do what you have to do, but we want him," the other voice said.

No specifics were mentioned, names were inflected, not enunciated. Their intent was obvious. We had an informer in the precinct. Internal Affairs euphemistically refers to them as "Field Associates."

Field Associates are recruited in the Police Academy. The motives of these young officers are of the highest order; they receive no extra compensation or special treatment. In fact, they may go through their entire careers with only one or two superiors at headquarters aware of their identities. When assigned to a precinct, they are directed to report anything that smells of corruption to a contact within the department.

On occasion, they are directed to take a good hard look at a specific individual or location.

Unfortunately, sometimes they also report innocuous happenings, bravado statements, and tall tales. The result is destructive to open and free communication. Nothing can put a damper on a precinct joker more than the news that he is under investigation for making certain statements. For example, Sergeant Muldoon, who always tries to introduce a laugh into the dry roll call training lessons, was instructing the platoon in self-defense. During the lecture he said, "If you really want to know how to use a blackjack, ask Sergeant Jones." This statement was reported to Headquarters. An investigation was conducted. The result: Sergeant Muldoon was directed to be more prudent when instructing the troops. Sure, Sergeant Muldoon has a lousy sense of humor, but did it call for an investigation? One can see why the men detest the system; it smacks of fascism. It also made Muldoon's lectures, once tolerable, unbearable.

While I am not opposed to rooting out corruption, I feel uneasy when one officer is given the specific job of nailing another officer. It goes beyond the feeling that these men are company finks. When you take on the job, you assume a public trust; if you screw up, you screw up. A lot has been said about cops covering up for other cops. But in uniform, you can't afford to work with a man who screws up; it's too dangerous. If a uniformed cop goes bad, he is eventually dismissed, and the reason for his dismissal is generally unprofessional conduct. We don't need spies to tell us when we're being unprofessional. We don't need hatchet jobs.

I hung up the phone and staked out the room where that particular extension was. A man I knew as Patrolman Mooney left after a while. I was shaken for a moment. He was well liked by the men and thought a competent officer by his superiors. Perhaps what he was doing would eventually contribute to the health of the Department. Since much police shop talk is generally irreverent, cynical, and provocative, I hoped he would be discreet. Shit, I remember thinking, we've got enough problems in the Four-one. The undercover operation seemed superfluous to me.

At 9 P.M., there was another car fire on Fox Street. Later, we responded to a call about an assault on three men in the same area. Their complaint: The firemen beat them with wrenches. I was convinced that these were the same men who had terrorized Harry Williams earlier. Moe called them "bad actors," which meant they were trouble, but there was no evidence on which to base an arrest. Since there had been two previous fires, very similar in nature, Moe figured the firemen were protecting themselves from harassment. "Score one for the good guys," he said under his breath as we turned the case over to the detectives.

Sergeant Saverin, as I had directed him earlier, decided it was time to move on the social club. He put himself out on the radio. Having second thoughts about my bureaucratic attitude, I decided to take a look too. Moe rolled up 170th Street, then gabbed a right onto Bristow.

Social clubs are legal. However, what goes on in them isn't always legal. Many clubs sell liquor without the required license; in some clubs drugs are available, in others prostitution or large-scale gambling. The precinct was saturated with them and it was our job to keep them under control.

Usually we just confiscate the booze, issue a summons, and leave. In this instance, the sergeant couldn't find the owner. It was his bust. I was learning. I kept my mouth shut.

Three patrolmen started dumping liquor bottles into garbage cans. Suddenly worried, the sergeant told them to put what they could into the radio cars.

"Shouldn't we take it all?" I asked.

"We should, but I don't think we ought to," he told me. Again I didn't think. Countermanding his order, I told the men to remove all the liquor. I was afraid that if we didn't take it all, it might look like we were taking a bribe.

"I want to make this as quick as possible," the sergeant said. "I'll give the summons to the guy with the keys." I said nothing. Later I realized that while I was worried about giving the appearance of a bribe, the sergeant was more concerned with maintaining some semblance of public order. But that was later.

Word soon spread that the first drunk of the weekend was being canceled. The neighborhood people gathered around the club. You sensed the questions being asked. Suspicion became rumor; rumor became fact. At that moment, there's no percentage in arguing the finer points of the law.

Cursing began when the sergeant questioned the man with the keys. He didn't want to take the rap for the owner, and he didn't want to lose the trade that meant his job. So he started shouting in that mixture of Spanish and English so endemic to the South Bronx.

Delay, though, might turn an incident into a riot. We could feel the tension building to some sort of resolution. When the man refused to identify himself, we arrested him. That started it.

Bricks and bottles began to fly. We got the prisoner out the front door and decided there wasn't much sense in sticking around. Moe had the engine running in my car when I turned toward it, but then the crowd cut me off.

My next move was toward the sergeant's car, and I felt my stomach heave when I saw the car moving away, lights flashing, through a fusillade of bricks and bottles. A rock struck me on the thigh. I dodged a flying Dr. Pepper bottle.

A black face pressed against mine. Sweating, his head ringed by a bandanna, the man screamed, "You motherfucker. If you didn't have the guns, we'd kill you." I believed him. At least three hundred people milled about me and not one had a blue shirt on.

"Look, we just want to give the gentleman a summons," I tried to tell them.

"That man don't run the place," a voice yelled back. "He works six days on a truck. Why are you motherfuckers arresting him?"

By that time, the crowd was angry, on the point of becoming a violent mob. But I knew if I drew my revolver, I was dead. So I challenged the mob's apparent leader.

"If you're not satisfied with the way we handled things," I told him, "come down to the station house and we'll straighten it out. We were only trying to give your friend a summons."

For a moment, the man was taken aback and his anger abated. I turned and pushed my way through the crowd. I knew how a toreador felt as he turned his back on a live, very angry bull. Am I in New York

City? I asked myself. Nothing in the Academy's training program could teach a man how to react properly in a situation like this. There were two loud cracks. Firecrackers. I jumped, and the crowd laughed. I made it to our car and slumped in the seat.

"Central, disregard the request for a 10-85 [meet a car] with two cars at Bristow Street," I heard Moe saying. He moved the car deftly through the crowd. Some bystanders jeered, others stared at us, their faces ashen and hard in the street lights. There was so much I had to learn, I realized, about police work in a ghetto. Strangely, I also realized that night, I wanted more than ever to stay in the Four-one and finally become a cop.

4

A COP QUICKLY LEARNS to begin with the end and work back to the beginning. Robberies, rapes, murders, muggings are all accomplished facts; reconstructing what happened is your main job. Only after some experience do you learn to cope with the antecedents: grief, anger, despair, loneliness. Most cops eventually realize that they spend most of their professional lives rummaging through the past, pulling apart old clothing, staring at yellowed, frayed photographs.

Of course, if a case takes any time, it passes into the hands of the detectives. At the scene, though, you reconstruct visions of the victim. How often had you seen him or her? Where? In whose company? What did he or she do? In some instances the answers are reflex. Many times, a few replies suffice. Then you pan the faces of the crowd, searching out a friend, an eager enemy. The pattern twists in counterpoint to the street: You are straight and out there is someone who is not. You want the bust, that hidden face responds with defiance. You deal with the ends and look for a beginning. Making sense out of the whole tangle of mired emotion is the only hope.

Take Cora Cruz.

Moe set me up for Cora. I had asked him to stop at a bodega for some Philly Perfectos. He stopped at the corner of Fox and Intervale and pointed at the store. I went in.

Behind the counter was an alert, neatly dressed woman in her late thirties or early forties. Her skin was dark, her body firm, mature. When I ordered my cigars she smiled and said hello, her eyes flashed with intelligence and a warmth that almost made me defensive. A semiprecious stone in a large ugly coal pit, I thought at the time.

Moe smiled slyly when I got back into the car. "Cora's nice, huh?" he said.

"So that's Cora," I said. "If only I was unhappily married." Suddenly things didn't seem quite so bleak. He shoved the car into drive and we glided down the street.

Darkness settled about us, and the heat became oppressive. I looked at the people as they thronged the street, drinking beer, playing cards and dominoes and realized that this was the end for many of them. There was no other place to go.

Life went its dusty way on the radio. "Four-one David. Respond to a disorderly group in the street at Seneca and Longfellow." We decided to pass. "Four-one Eddie. Respond to Kelly and Longwood. Two men trying to break into car." We would only get in the way there. The dispatcher's voice went up in pitch. "Four-one John. Respond to Hall Place and 167th Street. A stabbing in the street." We moved on that one.

On our way to the reported location, Moe said it was probably the gangs again. He was right. Siren on, dodging double-parked cars, doing the whole *French Connection* bit, we shot up Stebbins Avenue and turned right on 167th Street. About twenty-five kids – the word now seems anachronistic; they grow up early in the Four-one – split in all directions as we neared Hall Place. I spotted Sector John moving down Intervale

Avenue and yelled over the radio for them to grab a couple of those "kids."

One wasn't running. He lay face down on the sweaty, grimy street. No sound from him. Only eulogies for a street citizen could be heard: the screech of brakes, the wailing sirens, the obscenities, the shuffle of feet.

Sector Henry pulled up. "The kid's dead," one of the officers said to me as they bundled him into the back of the car.

"He's not dead until a doctor tells me that," I said, not in anger but frustration. "He's not dead unless he's in parts." The officer was right, I knew. But to give up hope is to join that kid and all the kids before him. What the hell, I figured, there's always a chance.

Later I learned he had been first stomped and then stabbed fourteen times. He didn't make it. That was the end and now we had to find a beginning. As we were getting into the squad car, Sector John grabbed a couple of kids who wore "Ghetto Stompers'" colors.

It figured. Hall Place and 167th Street is the northeast boundary of "the Stompers." The two in custody were clean so, unless we could come up with something else, the DA probably would not push charges on them. Frustration. An end and no beginning. I dispatched a car to the gang's hangout. Maybe they could find something.

We dug into the rubble of a young life. We found out that his name was Jesus Rosario. We also learned that he was a member of a rival gang, "the Savage Nomads." More of the beginning. His mother asked him to pick up her *bolita* (numbers winnings). He got off at the wrong bus stop and was rousted by the

47

Stompers. When he refused to give them the money, they attacked.

Money or no money, the Stompers probably would have gone after him anyway for trespassing on their turf. There was bad blood between the gangs and boundaries between the two were strictly adhered to. Moe was sure there would be a retaliation; it was a matter of who, where, when, and how many casualties.

In the late fifties, when *West Side Story* attained the peak of its popularity, the gangs declined in New York. Throughout the sixties, they were virtually extinct. Some saw drugs as the reason for their dissolution; others cited urban renewal and the shattering of the neighborhood as explanations of the decline. But by the beginning of the seventies, gangs were back in style.

They cordoned off their "turf." They swaggered up Southern Boulevard or 149th Street or Tremont Avenue dressed in jeans, their Levi jackets emblazoned with the gang name. They seemed belligerent, yet some were genuinely interested in attacking community problems. Most of the time, though, they attacked rival gangs. Community action became the community stomp. In the ensuing rumbles, it was impossible to distinguish the socially responsible from the irresponsible.

The resurgence of the gangs had stimulated media interest. A lot of them made TV. They cleaned this and that street. They drove so many pushers out of the neighborhood. No matter what they said under the TV lights, their presence lowered still further the ghetto's threshold for violence. Whatever the case, they were walking provocations, more threats to the precarious sanity of the streets. Rosario's death would be chalked up on a chart we keep on gang violence and the gangs would go on.

And then, just before we left the murder scene, Moe decided to do one of his numbers.

I was ready to leave but he stopped me. "I think we ought to ask the store owner to wash away the blood he said quietly. "Look, blood has an intoxicating effect on some people. It has a mysterious, almost hypnotic effect, bringing them to a fever pitch where an additional sacrifice is called for." I stared at him. Was this for real?

"I sense on these occasions the black magic of Haiti," he went on. "The witch doctor leading the ritual dance of death." I almost laughed, but then I looked at the crowd. I could feel something beginning to ferment; some of the people hung back and cursed us while others jumped and screamed and pressed forward. Moe's solemn intonation made the atmosphere eerie. He stood there, his erudition flowing out of his back pocket like some streetcorner sociologist, discussing cultural atavism. Fear, probably imagined, enveloped me. Then, with a gentle hissing sound, the bodega's owner washed down the sidewalk. I watched the blood slowly dissolve and then flow with the water into the gutter. That's where most of it goes. No dust into dust in the Four-one. Moe and I went back to the car, the fever seemingly broken.

The radio crackled on. Robbery in progress; burglary in progress; family fight in progress. We were going to have a backlog. Without the cars to answer all those calls, those deemed of lesser importance would have to be deferred. I left the sergeant to collect the final details of the homicide and asked Moe to head for the robbery in progress.

It was at a social club on Kelly Street. Social clubs are not the primary units of personal and political interdependence in the neighborhood. For such purposes, and several others, street corners do just as well. In a social club, recognized residents of a neighborhood, usually male, can get together to talk, drink, gamble, shoot pool, play cards, and, on occasion, work out personal differences. Their prime value is that social clubs do not have to observe the same laws bars do, and a stranger in their midst is easily identifiable, hence easily dealt with. Also, they keep a few people off the streets who might have made trouble. In a way, I suppose, we tended toward a hands-off policy as long as there were no flagrant violations of the law. Most of the calls we took from them involved debt, or a woman, or just some personal slight. Emotions generally ran high and initially most of the disputes were difficult to handle. After a few minutes, though, tempers would cool and voices lower. This call was an exception.

By the time we hit Kelly Street, Sector Henry was on the scene. Four males, they told us over the radio, had marched into the club armed with shotguns and proceeded to fleece not only the club but its patrons, and in a most undignified manner. Driving by, we could see a crowd of about thirty cursing people surrounding the squad car. Everything seemed to be under control; Sector Henry continued his broadcast calmly. Look for a green Chevrolet station wagon with New Jersey plates, he intoned.

Then a call came over the radio. "We've got them, they're heading south on Southern Boulevard." In the finest tradition of police procedure, the car in pursuit did not identify itself. If the report was accurate, we were in a position to intercept. Moe made a quick left onto Westchester Avenue, then flipped the car left again onto Intervale and moved toward Southern Boulevard.

In case you don't know the South Bronx, Southern Boulevard is not exactly a boulevard. Perhaps it earns its name by being wider than most of the other streets in the Four-one, or perhaps it is because it does not have an el to shadow its way between misery and squalor. Whatever prestige it possesses is found in the luxuriousness of the cars that double-park on either side of the street. But beyond the El Dorados and the Toronados and the LeSabres, the visitor's eye must focus on a tawdry line of gin mills, pizza parlors, and dry cleaning shops that more often than not are fronts for bookies or pushers. It begins in the Four-O at Bruckner Boulevard and snakes its way north like some great, atrophied vein, a mainline for the Four-one, punctured four, six, ten times too often.

What we didn't know at the time was that Patrolmen Sam Brick and Al Grant were roosting up on the elevated Sheridan Expressway, placidly handling an accident. They followed the chase over the radio. Brick, a large and jovial man, cursed his bad luck for missing out. Grant nodded and patiently filled out the lengthy report in which vehicle A, a large truck, side-swiped vehicle B, a car, at the end of the expressway while vehicle B was negotiating a sharp turn onto the Cross Bronx Expressway. Don't worry, Grant told his partner, there will be plenty of other opportunities.

By this time, we were closing in on the station wagon. It made a quick right on Longwood Avenue, circled back across Southern Boulevard, and then moved north on Bruckner Boulevard. Sector Charlie had stationed itself at Southern and Liggett Avenue. As the station wagon crossed Southern Boulevard for a second time, the squad car spotted it and roared off in pursuit. By chance, we were in a similar position, and when Moe hit Bruckner Boulevard we were only 15 seconds behind Sector Charlie.

The driver of the station wagon really poured it on. Undoubtedly he heard the squad cars in pursuit and decided to take evasive action. By now the Tactical Patrol Force had joined the chase. In and out of lines of traffic we swerved. As Moe pushed the car, I called in additional units to seal off possible exits. There was a chance the pursued might go on into the Four-three and I alerted that precinct. Lights flashed by like sparklers.

Suddenly the station wagon swerved from the middle lane, through the divider, and into the right lane. Sector Charlie alertly followed him, with one exception. He didn't make it. Coming north was Sector Frank. As the two squad cars collided, they formed a pillar of steel and crushed glass. Fortunately, the injuries were minor. But we had no choice about abandoning the chase.

The station wagon roared past Hunts Point Avenue and up onto the Sheridan Expressway. Patrolman Brick, still at work on the accident, had one ear cocked toward the radio. He figured the car would exit on Westchester Avenue and be home free. It didn't. It continued on, racing toward his position. Reacting quickly, Brick ordered those involved in the accident to get off the road. He and Grant pulled the squad car out on the turn, blocking it. They flipped on the turret light.

As the two cars, the pursued and the pursuing, came into view, Brick grabbed the radio and shouted at the Tactical Unit, "Slow down for chrissake, the curve is blocked." Seeing the flashing light, the driver of the station wagon increased his speed. Too late, the driver saw the disabled truck. He slammed on his brakes, skidded into the truck, and bounced over the guard rail into the Bronx River below, landing upside down. The radio car followed him over the edge.

By the time Moe and I reached the scene, a dozen cars had responded to the frantic calls. A patrolman named Rye dove into the murky waters of the river with the alacrity of some latter-day Tarzan. He emerged seconds later covered with mud: No one had told him that the water was only about a foot and a half deep. Grant found one of the officers in the darkness and pulled him to safety. In situations like this, I am often amazed at how well people improvise their responses. Moe, on his toes as usual, pulled our car to the edge of the road and trained the headlights on the pandemonium below. The second officer was okay. We groped in the water for the other four men. Stepping on something hard in the mud, Rye reached down, felt hair, pulled and came up with a severed head. He promptly fainted.

We were able to save two of the men from that station wagon. They were slightly drunk but otherwise in fairly good condition. Charges of robbery, resisting arrest, and reckless driving were lodged against them.

Back at the Fort, the complainants awaited us – all thirty of them. While most of the personal belongings and money had been recovered, they wanted restitution in blood. When they saw the two prisoners, all hell broke loose. The area in front of the sergeant's desk became a collage of shirts, fists, teeth, chains, and anguished faces. Sorting the sounds was even more difficult as the shouts, grunts, screams of pain, and muffled orders mingled together. I was glad I didn't have to live next to this crazy place.

Only when an officer pulled out his pistol and fired several shots into an already pockmarked ceiling were we able to seize the initiative and hustle the prisoners to safety. My face was bleeding. Why, I couldn't remember. I only knew that I was good and pissed. We lined the people up and had them searched. Result: 16 knives, 7 razors, 2 ice picks, and 30 smiles. When the patrolman got to the five women who were part of the group, he balked at the task. Later I was told that he had once been burned by a "female impersonator" in a Harlem bar only to find that the "he" was a genuine she.

As my anger slowly evaporated I was grateful for his hesitancy. Under departmental procedures, a policewoman must make such searches. Policewomen on patrol were still in the future. We didn't have time to get one here. And, I realized, I couldn't arrest them all. What for? Possession of a knife, a razor, or pick was against the law, but such possession is also a part of life in the Four-one. Bust them for adapting to the ghetto? An exercise in fatuousness. Disgusted that these people would bring such weapons into a station house, I told Moe to get them the hell out. The complainants were told to be in court in the morning. The end and the beginning. I squirmed inwardly over my rationalizations. Was it my business to make excuses? Eventually I decided that all I had done that night was save some lives and prevent some people from going to jail on homicide charges. The two men who died, incidentally, were not classified as homicides – their deaths resulted from their own negligence.

After my wounds were treated at Lincoln Hospital, I called my wife and asked her to wait up for me. A calm home, a quiet talk with her, and a scotch on the rocks seemed inviting and that prospect relieved some of the tension. When we returned to the precinct, Jerry Ardle, the attendant, asked us if we had time for some franks and beans. It wasn't exactly what I had in mind, but since we never know when we're going to have time to eat, we eat whenever we can. I told Jerry I would eat upstairs. I never got out of the muster room.

Through the front door stumbled a man later identified as José' Martinez. "They threw my son off the roof," he shouted. "I can't reach him. He's between two buildings." As I ran out the door with Martinez, another man came in who had been shot in the buttocks. Him, later. My mind was on the kid.

At 1015 Tiffany Street we found Phillip wedged between two buildings. His moans of fright and pain echoed upward. We summoned the emergency service. Luckily the boy had landed on a screen wedged between the buildings. Its presence saved his life.

Moe told me, "They're holding forty-six jobs now." His face grew taut. "Fat chance you'll get an answer on this one." I felt like putting my fist through the nearest wall.

Central advised us that the emergency service would be a few minutes; they were still trying to recover the body that matched the head plucked from the Bronx River. "The hell with it," I told them. "Forget about the dead one and save the live one."

When they finally arrived, the boy's cries had increased in intensity. A piece of the metal screen was imbedded in his back. He couldn't move. When he did, the piece imbedded itself still deeper.

We decided to go through a wall. The super let us in to an empty apartment and we cut through the wall above the bathtub. It was hard, hot work, but finally we were able to get to the kid. Although hurt and sobbing, the boy survived. Another senseless act chalked up on the slate of slum life. As often happens in the Four-one, I wondered if I should report the hole we had chopped through the side of the building, and then I forgot about it.

By that time, the dispatcher announced that he held fifty-four jobs in the Four-one. I asked the duty captain for assistance. Eight cars, four from the Four-three and the Four-five precincts, were dispatched to help with the workload. This was getting ridiculous.

Sweat seeped through my uniform as Moe pulled up at the station house. The world was ferociously dark that night. Our lives were measured by the lengths of blocks, by the number of fire escapes, by the depth of air chutes. We waded through broken glass and beer cans, through discarded furniture and discarded lives.

As I got out of the car, the man who had been shot in the buttocks walked by. Sergeant Welsh, relieving the station house supervisor for a meal, told me that he told the man to take a taxi to the hospital; no radio cars or ambulances were available. The guy simply picked a bad night to get shot. The radio crackled on.

"Man down – Vyse and 172nd Street – available Four-one car." There was no response. "Disorderly man in José's Bar on Fox Street – available Four-one car." No response.

Sergeant Saverin, a bulky man, his face softened by sweat, came lumbering through the door. "Hey, Lou, it's murder out there," he said. I almost said, "Do bears shit in the woods?" but even a tired joke like that would have been out of place. We were all exhausted. I felt like a general whose right and left have folded and whose center crumbles as he awaits the reinforcements he knows will never come. Cementing his desperation is the knowledge that there is no room for retreat.

I had three sergeants, Welsh, Saverin, and Bartow, in the field. After the fracas in the muster room, I wanted another sergeant on the floor, so I put Sergeant Welsh in command there. A few beers and the heat might bring that mob back.

Then an officer walked in with an eight-year-old boy; a woman followed them in. "What have you got?" Welsh asked. "Purse snatch," was the answer.

Right behind him came a young, intelligent, conscientious officer named Ruth. He had apprehended two fourteen-year-olds. This meant seven cars out of service. A monstrous equation ran through my head. To wit: More calls equaled more responses equaled more arrests equaled less cars on the street equaling fewer responses equaling a bigger backlog. About the only appropriate response I could muster was to hope that the franks and beans, if indeed there were any franks and beans left, weren't cold. But with over forty calls still unanswered, I'll have to wait for history's judgment.

"These are the kids that threw the Martinez boy off the roof," Ruth said.

"How did you get them?"

"I interviewed a couple of the boy's friends. They told me these two kids had been shaking him down in school. Phillip turned them into the principal and they decided to take revenge. They've been waiting for this chance all summer.

"The kid will be all right. Just a broken leg and arm." Ruth led the two to the desk. Just a broken leg and arm. The blessings of fortune in the Four-one. I looked at their faces. No feeling showed. They might just as well have thrown a mute doll down that air shaft. Didn't they feel the body squirm? Didn't they hear the screams? Didn't they feel at all? On the verge of smashing their heads together, I stepped back. Should I let them strip me of my humanity as well?

Once again the radio ended my thoughts. "Man shot – 996 Aldus Street." I heard Four-one Sector Ida take the job. Sergeant number two also responded. Moe stood by the door trying to attract my attention. I told Sergeant Welsh, who was waist deep in paperwork, to let go with a 10-1 (call your command) if he needed any help. Then I was out the door, grateful for the O/O idea. On my way to the car, Sergeant Bartow told me that he would give the eight-year-old purse snatcher a break. I nodded agreement. Bartow was sharp and I trusted his judgment.

Moe wasted no time moving out, but I told him to slow down. I was getting a little tense and I didn't mean to take it out on him. But it was my responsibility to see that everything was handled properly and everything in this precinct meant a helluva lot. Over the radio came more grim news: The dispatcher was now holding seventy-six jobs in the Four-one. Hell, some precincts don't even handle seventy-six jobs in

one day! I settled back and tried to form some semblance of control.

It started to rain. Not cool rain, not cleansing rain,
just the warm fitful rain that drives people off the
streets and into the bars and clubs and flats that frame
their lives. When it stopped the air would still be
heavy, the streets filthy, the lots cluttered. And we
would all sweat again.

When we got to Aldus Street, we found a young
man, lying on the street in a large pool of blood. Most
of his face had been blown away. "He's dead," a TPF
sergeant told me and I felt like commending him for
his perceptiveness.

One thing the TPF had learned was that the slay-
ing had something to do with narcotics. In this
neighborhood it was not exactly a bold assertion, but I
could deal with it. While we roped off the area, I noticed a nervous-looking man huddled on the periphery
of the scene. Impulsive judgments are infrequently
vindicated, I know, but sometimes you get a hunch
that feels like the reaction to a rap on the kneecap.
This was one of those hunches. Before I could act, the
crowd dumped on us.

I don't know what caused the reaction; usually we
never know. It might be a word misunderstood, a
threatening gesture. An instrument hasn't been in-
vented that can measure the volatility of a crowd
watching a police action. All I know is that a chunk of
concrete struck the top of the radio car. A second piece
followed, smashing the windshield of Sector Ida.
Bodies scattered, propelled by some indeterminate
force. A piece of metal caught Moe on the arm and he
went down, screaming. Quickly I hustled him across
the sidewalk and into a luncheonette.

Inside, I sat him in a booth and gabbed his walkie talkie. I gave a 10-85 (meet a car signal). This call is a disguised 10-13 (assist patrolman) which is held in reserve for a real crisis. In the Four-one the 10-13 is used only when we are in serious trouble; if guns are involved, if we are being attacked by a large group, or if we are injured and unable to defend ourselves. In this instance the crowd was menacing without being dangerous. I knew that they could become murderous at any moment, but the sight of patrol cars, lights flashing, sirens on, would scatter them. If the price paid was a few aches for Moe, we got off easily. I could see he would be all right so I went back out on the street.

The people were enjoying our predicament. The rain had stopped and down the asphalt street the water pooled and steamed and evaporated. Our uniforms felt sticky, cumbersome again with the heat. Patrolmen hit the roofs and found them empty save for some bricks and other objects suitable for filling a dark street. I told them to hold their positions until we were ready to leave.

Six cars responded to the scene and I told five of them to get back on patrol. A detective named Shane of the assault squad arrived and immediately perked my spirits. "Hey, Lou," he called, "every time you work, it really hits the fan."

I couldn't argue. Besides, I was glad to see Shane. A slim, pipe-smoking man, he had always impressed me as being careful, intelligent, and discreet, more like a scholar than a cop. Which was more than I could say of some of the other detectives in the district. Some of them couldn't be bothered with a problem if it wasn't self-serving. You always have those that look for the big case, the ones that will show up in the *Times* or the

News. Unfortunately the big case doesn't show up in the Four-one. A ghetto murder, unless it is bizarre or particularly savage, doesn't rate big headlines. Most readers don't want to know what is happening to the other half. Many innocent people, decent people, are killed in the Fort and nobody gives a damn about their passing except, maybe, their families and, always, the police. That's why I could appreciate a man like Shane.

During the bombardment, the TPF caught the man I had been watching and hustled him out of danger. His name was Ramon Guzman and Shane questioned him with patient persistence. Within minutes the connection emerged. Ramon admitted that he knew the dead man and that his name was Hector Garcia. A heroin purchase had been arranged between him and Garcia. Then the bullets spat out of the night. He was scared; he knew very little. I heard the same theme: The end is here, now find the beginning. That was Shane's job. Mine was to find other paths for him to pursue.

In this instance we got lucky. Most people at the scene of a homicide are hostile and uncooperative. Since many of our homicides are committed out on the street, this compounds the problem of witnesses and evidence. Usually, we learn little at first, then someone with information, after giving the matter some thought, wanders into the station house and gives up the perpetrator. This doesn't happen all the time, but it does explain our 86 percent clearance rate in homicides.

As we waited for ballistics, photo, and the lab to go over the scene, I looked for Moe. He was up and chatting with his friends in Sector Ida, an officer nicknamed "the bird" and the other, Kowalski. Moe was cursing the bastard on the roof. He was bruised –

more psychologically than physically, which made me happy. I had seen other men, less close to me than Moe, seriously injured by trash thrown off a roof. He shrugged off the pain and we got back into the car. The night seemed endless. We were in a slender, darkened corridor whose only exits were locked doors. Occasionally the latch would be drawn back, the door opened briefly, and we would witness acts of terrible, gross violence. Then the door shuts again. If I had nightmares (which I was too tired to have) this would be one of them.

Leaving the scene., Moe grabbed a right on Hoe. He finally realized how close he had come and I could see his face tense suddenly. Incidents like these meant recurrent memories for most cops. The mind, at times, reshuffles itself like a deck of cards and then the memories reappear; the faces screaming, the faces distorted with fear and hate, and the faces simply dead.

A woman appeared above us, bizarrely clad in a coat of soap suds. She hung out a window cursing with enough gusto to attract our attention.

"That bastard has done it again," she shrieked. Her screams followed us up the stairs.

Was it a kinky sex act perpetrated by a man with an obsession for cleanliness. Had Mr. Clean invaded her bathtub without asking first? Had someone devilishly slipped detergent in her martini shaker? Moe and I ceased our speculations when we reached the apartment and the woman answered the door wrapped in a red towel. "That son of a bitch has shut off my water again," she yelled. Who? "That sonuvabitchin' super. He's always shutting off my water."

Moe listened and then told her we'd look into the matter. From the look on his face, I knew he saw an early solution. "I've seen some like this before," he said as we went down to the basement.

It was full of water. Some junkies had cut away all the pipes and copper tubing – anything of value was fair game for them. The woman followed us partway down the stairs and Moe tried to console her. She remained beyond consolation. "Why the hell I come up here?" she said. "I have more dignity back home. At least my husband stay home."

We notified the super and the Department of Water Supply, Gas and Electricity.

The radio hadn't stopped. The dispatcher requested a car for a robbery long past, a suspicious man loitering in front of a bar, an alarm ringing at a factory. Moe wanted to roll on the alarm. He enjoyed climbing onto factory roofs, tracking down trespassers. It was the ironworker in him – his moonlighting specialty. I told him to forget it. On a night like this, even burglaries become petty crimes.

I began to realize the strain this workload put on a man. An enormous number of jobs lurched toward us, and few were exactly simple. I had the luxury of rolling on the jobs that interested me, but I could still feel the pressure. Yet they responded, call after call, the same patient voices acknowledging that they were on their way, that they had finished the job. What scared me most was when the voice turned strident and the 10-13 rasped over the air. I never got used to it.

As we pulled up in front of the station house, the radio bleeped, "Sector Boy, respond to the Tiffany Street dock – man on water." One of the sectors was needling an ex-seminarian, Joe Hinds, in Sector Boy.

I could have said something but I didn't. A voice came over the speaker, "Maybe it's Jesus Cruz."

Another voice whispered over the air. "Have Sergeant Saverin respond – they can take a walk together." I laughed. Crude, sophomoric, I wasn't worried. Laughs still separated the men from despondency or, worse, despair. And our relative efficiency remained unimpaired. I think I needed the rebound as much as the men did.

When we went inside, the fourteen-year-olds involved in the Martinez incident were about to be released in their parents' custody. They were youthful offenders and it was doubtful that they would see much hard time for what they had done. A couple of years at Wiltwyck, a reformatory, perhaps, then back out on the streets, tougher than before.

One parent, Mr. William James, seemed genuinely upset. I told him to see Patrolman MacGlick, our community relations man. A karate expert, Mac is justifiably proud of the martial arts class he runs at P.S. 113. Maybe his program could help young James. I also suggested that James find some new friends. Even at that young age, I knew his possibilities of survival were marginal at best. I just couldn't ignore the situation.

The other father, Claude Howard, presented problems. He accused us of picking on his son because he was black. I asked him if he really believed that. He said yes, I'm sorry, but the guy got my goat. I felt my men made a good arrest and that it would be vindicated in the courts. To hang objections on the slender nail of racial prejudice was absurd in this case. I sensed it was only a question of time before his child would stand before my desk again. Weigh one against the other, I told myself, and hope that you'll never see William James again in this station house.

Sergeant Bartow came in and handed a report to the 124 man. (The 124 man types reports and processes complaints that come in from the field. The "124" comes from the section of the rules that authorizes the position.) "I didn't see you at the attempted suicide," Bartow said to me.

"I didn't know we had one."

"And I was beginning to think you were Superman."

Just then an officer walked through the door with another suspect. Bartow and I looked at him and then at each other. The eight-year-old purse snatcher.

"He tried to pick the pocket of a woman on the bus," the officer told us.

Dismayed, Bartow turned to me and said flippantly, "See what happens. I was trying to be a soul brother and you were trying to be a liberal and see where it got us." The kid looked at us mutely. We could bandy about all the psychological and sociological terms we knew; they wouldn't mean a thing to the boy. His eight-year-old world was remarkably well defined. You either made a hit or you got busted. That's life.

This time he would get no breaks. First he would be funneled into the appropriate agency, then into a juvenile correction facility. And then he would be back, I knew, and all too soon his face would blur, melt with all the others that shuffled past the desk sergeant. For a moment the beginning and the end teeter-tottered. I was seeing both and I didn't like what I saw. I looked away.

Forty-five minutes remained for the shift. A rough night – five dead bodies, two homicides. Ordinary jobs still rasped over the radio. Peeling open a cigar, I poured a cup of coffee and sat down behind the desk.

Then the dispatcher's voice rose as he called for an available Four-one unit. "Possible homicide at 172nd Street and Boone Avenue," the dispatcher said. I decided to hold my ground. If they needed me, they would call.

They needed me.

Four-one Sector Robert took the call. The men in the car and the dispatcher traded calls back and forth. One officer had a brogue as thick as a pint of stout. "That's Carey, Xavier Carey, from County Cork," the sergeant told me. The Irish, a Department cliché. But they, and myself included, seemed inseparable from the Department. Great, stolid, beefy men whose feet possessed an irresistible itch for the sidewalks of the city. Corrupt or clean, the basic model for a New York cop was still Irish.

Carey came back on. "Would you have the lieutenant respond to this location – we have a messy one." His voice never wavered. "It appears to be the body of a nude, decapitated Negro male."

I put my coffee down. Moe and I hit the street. I couldn't shrug off a feeling of deep depression. What kind of world is this? "They're not happy with wiping each other out," Moe said without smiling. "They gotta take a souvenir."

Arriving at the scene, we found that Carey had managed to understate the situation. Not only was the body apparently that of a nude, decapitated Negro male. It was the body of a *huge*, nude, decapitated Negro male. It lay half in the gutter and weighed about

300 pounds. During my days at the police laboratory, I had seen many victims of many hideous crimes; I turned my head on only three of them. This, it appeared, would be the fourth.

But as I started to turn from the corpse, I noticed something peculiar about it and managed to overcome my nausea to lean over for a closer look.

At that moment, Dr. Nim, from Lincoln Hospital, came by after answering a call. I asked him to look at the wounds. He patiently examined the corpse as mobile units, out of curiosity, drifted by for a look. I let them have a quick glimpse and then I shooed them back to their respective sectors.

After five minutes, Dr. Nim solemnly stood up as if to address an eager class of first-year medical students. "I'm sorry, gentlemen. Or perhaps I should say I'm glad," he said. "But you only have half a homicide." He cleared his throat while we all wondered what the hell he was talking about.

"This happens to be the body of a skinned gorilla." If the same three words ever collectively entered the minds of a group of men gathered together in common purpose, this was the time. I counted at least five who said simultaneously, "What the shit?" Then we realized that we stood only a block away from a large meat-packing plant. Carey regained his sense quickly; I could see he was sergeant material. "It must have fallen off one of their trucks when it made a sharp turn," he said.

Another man moaned, "Crap, I've been eating their hot dogs for years. No wonder the foreman smiled whenever he gave me a package. The bastard." Now it was their turn to feel sick.

I notified the city health department, the ASPCA, and the New York Zoological Society. I toyed with the idea of asking the detectives for a rundown on men with records that indicated an M.O. (method of operation) for gorilla-nabbing, but I didn't think I would have much luck. I was right. Six months later we found a skinned bear at the same location. A spate of grizzly jokes swept the Four-one. In the meantime, I swore off hot dogs.

Our reports filed, the day shift mustered, I headed for home. On nights like this I felt like an anonymous street sweeper whose badge is his broom and whose dustpan is his only weapon. Driving north, past all those mute, shuttered buildings, I could only guess at what was going on inside. In most instances, I figured I didn't want to know. All I knew was that I would have a stiff scotch and go to bed. And then tomorrow I would wake up and return to the Four-one.

5

THE PROVING GROUND of the Four-one is Fox Street. Patrolling that street, you have to resist alternating feelings of nausea and claustrophobia. Apartment buildings, their windows tinned over, their interiors gutted, line the street like blind, blinkered beggars. Yet people live there, alongside the rats and the roaches. And like the rats and the roaches, they scurry furtively among the crumbling bricks and cinderblocks, almost as if movement itself were their only possible declaration of life.

Everywhere there is garbage. It lies in heaps, in lots, on stoops, on sidewalks, in the gutters. It accumulates, rots, rusts, disintegrates, and never seems to disappear. Wild dogs forage through it, children play in it, adults kick it aside. The Sanitation Department works many hours to remove it, but it always returns, almost as if it were some sort of collective sweat exuded by the neighborhood.

People too are strewn along the street, and this seems like a savage thing to say, but it is true. In the summer's fecund heat, the older people collect on street corners while the youngsters hang out windows or throng around open fire hydrants.

You sense the violence, but you don't realize its depth until a can or bottle comes hurtling out of the night and caroms across the hood of your car. Let that happen night after night and that car becomes a refuge; the radio your link with civilization and sanity. No way, you tell yourself, could you ever live like this.

Yet each day you watch thousands of people, many of them decent human beings, live exactly that way.

I run down the list of problems confronting Fox Street residents and it expands to frightening proportions. Youths, many of them homeless, band together and populate the cellars of buildings. Graffiti becomes a form of civic improvement. Even the rats challenge you as they scamper in front of the car, hissing at the headlights. Everything hangs out here and within weeks you've seen it all happen: people dying, shot, stabbed, beaten, bitten, poisoned, pushed, raped, run over, and, saddest of all, forgotten. Those that remain are just desperately playing out their string, waiting to see which guise death will take when it touches them. Welcome to Fox Street.

Our community representative, Mac, was in the Community Relations Office rapping with some kids. He's the officer designed to smooth things out between the precinct and the neighborhood. He also tries to spot problems before they arise. In this instance, he was attempting to arrange a truce between these gang members and another gang called the Ghetto Stompers. Peace between the two gangs would take an act of high diplomacy and he had dreams of brilliant success. After an hour-long discussion, the boys left and walked back toward their headquarters, a cellar on Fox Street.

Then all that patient work went down the drain. On the street they met Pepe, their armorer. He had encountered a man named Gonzalez on Southern Boulevard. An argument took place. Gonzalez accused Pepe of making a pass at Gonzalez's pretty wife. When Pepe angrily rebutted the charge, Gonzalez slapped him. The gang held a hurried meeting and agreed that the slap had indeed been an insult that demanded revenge.

Armed with shotguns and knives, they stormed into Gonzalez's apartment. First they tied him to a chair and forced him to watch as they repeatedly raped his wife. Then they cut her savagely with their knives. Finally, they placed a shotgun between her legs and pulled the trigger. Perhaps he felt some sense of gratitude when they turned the shotgun on him and papered the wall of the apartment with parts of his arms and chest.

Mac stood by the station house door as the kids were brought in. He thought he had reached them, he told me. I wondered in return: At what age do we lose them in this precinct, at seven, six, maybe even five? When does whatever spark of innocence that may have existed become lastingly tarnished? That day, I rode through the streets seething inwardly, waiting for some minor incident to irritate me, to bring this red rage to the surface. Fortunately, this was a quiet shift and I cautioned myself not to let the incident affect me this way.

Sometimes, though, the gangs displayed odd quirks of behavior that almost made them seem endearing.

The anti-crime unit had been keeping tabs on one of the other street gangs. Rumors about a possible rumble rattle through the area like a careening garbage can lid. One night, a gang moved casually off its turf toward Fox Street. The unit followed them. As the gang entered a cellar on the 600 block, back-up units were called for. We responded and edged slowly forward. Policemen, after all, are trained to be suspicious.

So we moved closer and then edged our way into the cellar. We heard yelling and screaming from behind the closed door. "This is it," I said to myself, and banged open the door. "Police," I shouted, "knock it off." A dozen men poured into the low-beamed room that was filled with cigarette smoke. The kids looked up, startled, then scared. We had them cold.

In the silence that followed, we suddenly heard the dulcet tones of "Maria" from *West Side Story*. Startled, we looked at a television set at one end of the room and found ourselves face to face with Leonard Bernstein's romanticized Jets and Sharks. The crew we followed that night had come to watch and cheer a re-run of the movie version. But they were ages apart from those fictionalized gangs. Violence to them meant blood spent, not celluloid expended. But we had nothing on them, so we curtsied back out the door, our faces blushing. The times you guess wrong are the times you remember.

Violence moved casually down Fox Street like an idle pickpocket looking for an easy mark. One day Moe, in the station house, patiently questioned a six-year-old. "Why did you do it?" he asked.

"He took my Devil Dog."

The boy paused and then plunged on. "That was my lunch. He had his."

We couldn't locate either mother and we took the wounded child, a four-year-old, to Lincoln Hospital. He had been stabbed in the chest for stealing a Devil Dog. Such is the value of life, appraised so early on Fox Street.

If anything, most kids were victims, up to a certain, statistically unspecified, age. You know their capacity for violence, but what kid in the city hadn't grown up with it? Yet you also sensed this sudden, awful destruction of their innocence.

Take this kid who ran when Moe and I spotted him. Moe chased him and caught him. His name was Freddie. We weren't sure why he had run except that he was very young, and very small and alone in the street. Eventually we learned that he had run away from home; his stepmother beat him constantly. That was when we noticed his strangely twisted arm.

We took him to Lincoln and a quick X-ray revealed that the arm was broken in two places. We contacted the appropriate agencies. I only hope they found a decent home. Maybe we had averted some suffering in the Four-one. Later, when I remembered Freddie, I thought of three-year-old Debbie and her cigarette-burned body; two-year-old Jimmy, mutilated by a machete; eighteen-month-old Carol, smothered to death; five-year-old Billy, thrown from a roof, and seven-year-old Victor, stomped to death. Even now, the names evoke anguished faces.

A six-year-old girl was missing. We were especially concerned because a nine-year-old girl had disappeared from a nearby location and was later found murdered. We headed to the apartment to get some information from the mother.

Entering the building, we were hit immediately by the dank air, strongly laced with the scent of urine. Eau de Bronx you might call it. Empty wine bottles, bottle caps, matches, beer cans littered the steps and landings. Two winos sat comfortably in the first floor corridor, guardians of one of the Four-one's many entrances to Hell.

All the windows we passed were broken. Even the paint and plaster had succumbed to the building's atmosphere; the paint was peeling off, chunks of plaster lay on the floor. Going up the stairs was a precarious business; large sections of marble were missing from the steps. Dogs barked from behind each door. And each door was sealed with layers of wood or steel, although I couldn't help thinking that there was probably little difference between what was being kept out and what was being kept in.

It took the woman several minutes to unlock all the hardware she had attached to the door. The apartment wasn't in much better shape than the halls. We asked the routine questions – the child's description, her age, when was she last seen, did she have a favorite place where she liked to go? We did it in flat monotone as though avoiding fear. Actually, I suppose it was boredom: We had played this scene so many times before.

Finally, I asked her if the super ever cleaned the halls. She laughed. "Go talk to him, you'll see." Our visit had upset the ecological balance of the apartment. Cockroaches and other bugs, irate over the disturbance, scampered across the walls. I opened the oven and found two mice hanging by their tails. It would have been nice to think that the kid had successfully gotten away from this, but we knew it was unlikely.

Downstairs, we ran into the super. When I first saw him, I reached for my gun, but he said I didn't need it. A muscular, 290-pound man, he was a convicted murderer out on parole. He patrolled the building with a machete in one hand and the leash of a German shepherd in the other. He looked after several buildings on Fox Street, and he told us the mother wasn't bad. Just desperate, I thought. Looking at him, I wasn't surprised to learn that everyone paid the rent on time.

We worked all night on this one, searching abandoned buildings, knocking on doors, visiting relatives, and coordinating the various units involved. We had just about given up hope when the youngster walked up Fox Street unhurt. Apparently she overstayed a visit to a friend's house on St. John Avenue. The searching and the waiting had been worth it.

Other violence took a more calculated stance. No one was immune, not even the modest housewife who wanted to shore up her budget with fifty cents on what she thought was her lucky number or $2 on a horse she felt had long legs. Gambling was a way of life to the people of the Four-one since they gambled with their lives every day.

So Big George did quite well for himself. His policy business boomed; his friends regarded him highly. Each afternoon, he sat in his apartment awaiting the arrival of his collectors. As they came in, he accepted their packages and began counting. While he checked on things, the collectors would go to the kitchen, grab a beer, and come back to watch.

The only sound to be heard during this time was Big George's footsteps as he moved between a table in the front room and the tab kept in the kitchen. This particular day, George seemed annoyed.

He called for José, and when the collector came into the kitchen, George pointed to the tab. José saw trouble coming. George had a simple system for collecting from recalcitrant female clients. Once their bill hit $50, he would request an audience, in his apartment, with her. The client would have to pay one way or the other. In this instance, the client was a Mrs. Ramirez, which made José nervous. He didn't think she would buy the solution.

But José had his job to protect so he went out and found Mrs. Ramirez. He made an appointment for her with Big George on a Friday night around midnight. She arrived at about 2 A.M. after attending a party with her husband. Apparently she wasn't impressed by George's legendary charm, became incensed by his suggestions, and attempted to leave. Unable to make a sexual conquest, George beat her up, mercilessly.

At 2:30 A.M. we received a call from Central. "Shots fired, Fox and 156th Street." We arrived to find a large crowd in the street. Apparently we had broken up a showdown between George and Mr. Ramirez. Some neighbor, knowing of the trouble, called 911. From experience they know that the quickest way to get us is to say that shots are being fired.

The next morning, Big George spotted Ramirez. He didn't waste any time. He drew a .375 magnum and blasted away. Alas, his aim, like his charm, had deserted him. He hit Ramirez in the toe, twice. The incident would have been funny except that his wild shooting brought down two innocent bystanders. One of them died. That ended Big George's career. Ironically, Mr. Ramirez has since taken over George's operation. It is reported that Mr. Ramirez has also adopted Big George's method of collecting from female debtors. Never let a good thing go to waste – it's the American way.

But usually, the violence on Fox Street remained random, often pointless. Terrible acts of desperation. There were times, though, when I felt there was simply no excuse.

We responded to the 800 block of Fox Street. As we entered the apartment, the distraught mother led us to a crib in the bedroom. There we found an unconscious, thirteen-month-old girl named Cindy. Patrolman Moritz gave the baby mouth-to-mouth resuscitation as a car sped them to the hospital. But she was dead on arrival. Another red stamp on yet another yellow form. The doctor found that the child had been severely beaten over a period of months. When arrested, the common-law husband screamed at his wife, "I told you to throw the little bitch out the window."

The trick to dealing with Fox Street, I learned, was not to distinguish between genders. As a man, as a cop, I tended to pull up a little short when talking to women involved in crimes. On Fox Street, though, many women were not only instigators but participants in crime. They did the assaulting, they did the beating, and, in some instances, they did the killing.

We headed up Southern Boulevard toward the station house for some steak and potatoes. On the day tour, you usually ate in the field. But few decent restaurants remained open at night and the constant threat of armed robberies made it difficult to relax in them.

As we approached Leggett Avenue, a group of small boys waved at us. We pulled up. One of the kids shouted, "There's a crazy lady running around on Fox Street." I almost laughed. On reflection, it is easy to see why the Four-one would shake anyone out of his or her tree. Lord knows, it's happened to enough cops.

We had to check it out. Making a right turn onto Fox Street, we encountered a large group of people. They laughed and chatted easily. When we asked what was happening, a woman pointed up the street and said, "She lives on the next block."

I told Moe to drive the car slowly up the street. I walked alongside. By walking, the faces of those on the street assumed more distinction. A hand slipping inside a jacket became a reach for a muscatel bottle and not a grasp for a hidden knife or pistol. I sensed little hostility in this crowd, though. It was almost as if they were intent on watching the denouement of a minor family comedy. The kind you usually watch through shrouds of laundry hanging in a dark airshaft between apartments. A scene from Celine's black vision of Paris, too desperate to be altogether serious.

We spotted a huge woman with five children, all carrying what appeared to be kitchen knives, as they disappeared into a tenement. Unable to locate them, we sought information. A family dispute, one man told us. He grinned; it wasn't serious. The crowd outside refused any additional information.

As we got back in the car, Moe observed that there were a lot of junkies in the laughing crowd. I noted this and tried making the connection. Then, as we moved toward the station house, the radio cracked, "Man shot, Leggett and Fox Street." Moe made a U-turn and headed south again.

By the time we got there the same crowd awaited us. A Transit Authority sergeant was on the scene and told me that one of his cars had taken the wounded man to Lincoln Hospital. Sector Eddie was also there and I started to dispatch them to the hospital to begin the investigation. Then along comes the huge woman and her five children and the crowd's mood shifted perceptively.

Cursing the crowd in Spanish, they stopped and scanned the faces. Then one of the younger children pointed a finger at a man. Eerie. Death making a skeletal gesture wearing the disguise of a seven-, perhaps eight-year-old girl. I stood planted on the spot.

Knives appeared from beneath a dress. They charged the man the girl had pointed at. No charges were made, no questions asked. It was ghetto law in its finest hour. You try to "off" me, and my family and friends will "off" you.

Later I would marvel at the way those children handled the knives. They were determined and cool and quick. Had they practiced? Who trained them? Considering the waste of talent would only be a superfluous exercise. Instead I chased them.

We managed to separate the group from their target. One patrolman, a man named Hyde, drew the toughest assignment – the mother. He disarmed her with an expertise I admired. I caught two of the youngsters and told them to drop their weapons; the girl complied, the boy remained belligerent. I walked toward him and repeated my order to drop the knife. He pointed the knife at my throat; his eyes reflected hate, fear, and confusion. The kid was really psyched up.

Once again, I gave the order to drop the knife. This time, he let the weapon go. The tough facade crumbled and he started to tell me about his father and his family's problems. He began to cry. But he hadn't gotten very far into his story when his mother raced over and knocked him to the ground. Before we could restrain her, she cursed him in Spanish and repeatedly kicked at him. "'Tell him nothing," she said over and over.

Later I tried to talk to the youngster, but he refused to say anything. The father, shot five times, also clung to this fierce code of silence. I never did find out what really happened that night. All I know is that some strange drama of violence and revenge was played on

Fox Street that night. Moe and I kept an eye on that block for a long time. We found we shared a strange feeling of admiration and pity for that family.

———————

Something very unusual was happening that night on Fox Street. I told Moe without mentioning any specifics. He shrugged and said he hadn't noticed anything unusual. Here grew a pile of garbage, the area's only natural vegetation. There sat a curbside game of dominoes, one of many local recreational centers. Moe went on. Grab a can of beer in a small paper bag and you're a one-person social center. Help your neighbor's wife into bed and you're a welfare worker; rob a bodega and you're contributing to the economic vitality of the area. Write your name on a wall and you're an artist, an instant celebrity. Moe could go on and on. But I had learned that his cynicism masked a real dedication to his job. Show him a resident wanting to help himself and Moe would give him his shirt.

"You've done it again, Watson." I told him, "You've seen everything but the obvious." Moe looked puzzled. "When was the last time," I said, "we drove down Fox Street and you didn't notice anything special. Never – that's it. The absence of anything unusual indicates that something extra special is going to happen."

He gave me one of those "You've-worked-too-many-evening-shifts-in-the-Four-one" looks and drove on. I believed my hunch though, and was determined to play it. Moe circled the blocks in a holding pattern while I drew up a course of action.

Back to the station house, I decided. I wanted to use Figua and Ramos, two of our Spanish-speaking officers on patrol. After briefing, they left in civilian clothes to investigate the blocks on Fox Street between Prospect and Longwood. As they left, Moe made the sign of the cross and smiled pontifically. Moe thought I relied on psychic impulses too often and this was another example. Frequently, facts verified his opinion. The times I was correct more than made up for my numerous failures. It also made the tour fun, a justifiable end in itself.

By Four-one standards, it was a quiet night. No unusual murders, robberies, or rapes occurred. One shooting got to Moe. The woman involved was Cora Cruz, who ran the bodega at the corner of Fox and Intervale. Her charge was firing a pistol at a robber who was holding up her husband. She didn't hit the man, but then she didn't have a permit to shoot the weapon at him. It cost her $1,000 to beat the case in court. Moe felt that her story was symbolic of the price that the decent people in the area had to pay to survive. What disturbed me was that they had to break the law to survive. There's no percentage in that.

Moe asked facetiously if I wanted to cruise up Fox Street again? "No hurry," I told him. "Let the boys have a little time to do their thing. They'll be calling us." An hour later, the call came through. "Four-one lieutenant, 10-85 [meet] portable unit at Fox and 156th Street."

Greeting us at the scene was a man who looked like a junkie. He wore sneakers, his pants and jacket had never gotten as far as a rinse cycle, and his face was a mask of wrinkles and watery eyes. It was my man Figua. He kept to the shadowy side of the car.

"Something going on in the basement of 574," he whispered. "It's an occupied building but the basement is sealed off for renovations. I've seen a lot of activity in and out of the place."

I had discovered that although he was very streetwise, he had no conception of police procedure. He'd go busting into a place without backup units. He used his nose instead of his head. In the words of a wise hacker, he was a great dribbler, but he didn't know when to pass off. Still, he was a valuable man if properly used. That night, he played the role he enjoyed most; the bloodhound picking up the scent of the criminal. In that role, I liked having him around.

I called for two more units and we moved in quietly. Figua had picked up the knocking code used to open the door. He quietly tapped out the progression of beats. The door opened and closed quickly behind him. Unbelieving, we stood out in the darkness.

"That son of a bitch," I yelled at Moe. "He's done it again. Get the door."

We had no alternative but to break through the entrance. We could hear the turmoil inside. No doubt, Figua had scored the touchdown. Now we had to find out if he had been hit and fumbled.

Moe took the door with his charge. We found Figua on the floor wrestling with two middle-aged Puerto Ricans. They cursed each other in Spanish. Over 250 men must have been in the place and they were all trying to leave by the same window at the same time.

What we were in the process of doing was busting up the Bronx's largest, floating cockfight. Billed as the championship of Fox Street, it featured a South American cock versus the pride of Puerto Rico with thousands of dollars at stake. Figua attempted to capture the cocks but the owners objected. Arrest didn't concern them; they were worried about their birds, valued at $2,000 each. A van was stationed in the rear and plucked off the men when they made it out the window. My hunch had been right, but I wasn't happy. I'd trade ten of this type of arrest for one robber or rapist. The ASPCA took the birds; the court fined the men.

We responded to the 1100 block on Fox. A young woman directed us to the apartment. As we walked up the stairs, we saw a young Puerto Rican man hanging by a sheet from the second floor landing. He was dead by the time we got there.

He was married with two children. When he asked for a pay raise from his employer, he was fired. At that time, he made $67.50 a week. He and his wife argued and she told him, "We can make out better without you." She was right. The family could make more on welfare. But would they be better off? Apparently he answered the question for himself as he wrapped the end of the sheets around his neck and flung himself over the railing.

Several officers and an ambulance attendant were carrying out three bodies as we arrived at 900 Fox Street. "What the hell happened?" I inquired. Patrolman Ruth responded, "It was just a bunch of junkies fighting over the split on the narcotics, nothing worth worrying about." "How are they?" I asked. "One's DOA and the other two look like they might go out of the picture," the attendant responded. The woman in the apartment next door, standing in her doorway listening to the attendant, crossed herself and said softly, "Thank God."

Some on Fox Street try to defend themselves, often with disastrous results.

José Gomez had owned a bodega on Fox Street for many years. The victim of several robberies, he bought a shotgun. A young black man, an addict and neighbor, tried to hold up Gomez with a knife one Saturday afternoon and got himself blown away. The word spread quickly through the neighborhood and, as usual, the word was distorted. It claimed the young man was assassinated.

A short time before this, a black resident had been killed by a sniper on the same corner. Fox Street logic assumed a relationship between these two shootings. The word got back to José. He closed up shop and left.

In the meantime, a posse formed. When they arrived at the store and discovered it empty, they decided to loot it. Someone set fire to the place. I didn't seem to bother the looters that many of their members lived in the building above the store. Justice, after all, must prevail.

Moe and I arrived on the scene and found several cops trying to control the crowd as firemen went after the blaze. Ten firemen were inside the store accompanied by thirty neighbors stuffing bags, pockets, and shirts with meat, vegetables, and canned goods. Those outside cheered them on.

I stopped two men from walking off with the cash register. A fire lieutenant moaned, "We're trying to fight a fire. Do your job, will you?"

Hearing him, a patrolman named Roark said, "Yeah, we know your problem. You like to shop alone."

I had to laugh. Roark was sent to round up some barriers. Once a secure perimeter was established, I could flush the people from the store. In all, six of us faced nearly two hundred people.

One man standing outside was yelling, "Burn, baby, burn." A woman hanging out a third floor window was screaming at the man, "You stupid bastard." It was his wife. Even with the tension we couldn't help laughing. The firemen did an excellent job, bringing the fire under control before it got past the second floor.

The crowd still swelled; they sensed a looting spree. Perhaps my energies would have lessened slightly if I knew Gomez robbed or ripped off his neighbors and cheated on his taxes, but I don't think so. Any cop or fireman on the line that night would have gone into any apartment and done his best to save lives and property. You can't afford to make absolute distinctions. What you do is try to keep personal pain at a minimum. Then you ferret around for all the broken pieces.

Curses came from the crowd. Several bottles hit the ground in front of us. "They're on the roof," some people yelled. "Watch the roof." Momentarily, the ploy worked. The operators of the radio cars backed away from the front of the store to protect their vehicles. I ordered them back and had barriers repositioned on either side.

Retreat, I knew, would be regarded as a sign of weakness. Weakness invited further attacks. You have to maintain that front of strength. A semblance of weakness must be avoided as much as overreaction. It's like chess, where a weakness in your pawns can lead to early defeat. So you clench your teeth and brandish a stick, hoping you'll never have to use it.

Eventually, I sent two men to the roofs as a precaution. Then I called in our anti-crime unit. Anti-crime was another of Commissioner Murphy's innovations. Each precinct was allowed to use five percent of its men in civilian clothes to fight street crime – robberies, muggings, assaults. These men weren't plainclothesmen; vice, gambling, and narcotics arrests were frowned upon. Serious street crime was their target. In my opinion, Sergeant Bannon had put together the best anti-crime unit in the city. In situations like this, I always felt a little more confident knowing they could be called on.

Sergeant Orange, myself, and several of the newly arrived anti-crime personnel moved out into the street. In problems of crowd control, it's best to be assertive, but not aggressive. I realized that I draw a fine line, but a cop in the street always has to sense how far he can push people when they are disrupting public order, but not committing clear-cut violations of the law. I don't object to crowds or demonstrations; I just don't like to see them turn violent. When push comes to shove and shoves lead to fists and bottles and, worse, gunfire, no one wins the point of the argument.

One man did toss a bottle at us. We moved quickly through the crowd, arrested him, and hustled him off. Then we split the crowd and drove them toward the ends of the block. Then we heard several sharp noises, the kind of cracks that make you duck instinctively.

That was when I noticed Patrolman Roark removing the stock of a weapon from the back of his trousers. Standing in a doorway, he took a plastic cap off the end. In the hollow butt of the weapon was a shotgun barrel and ammunition.

Moe nudged me. "That's guy's a corker." I nodded, but I wanted him off the street. I went over and told him to put the weapon away. There have been situations when I could have used a gun like that, but this wasn't one of them. I warned Roark not to carry it again.

I regrouped the men around the store. The crowd seemed quieter now. I asked the sergeant and two radio cars to stand by in case there were any further attempts at looting. Patrolman Roark was not requested to remain behind.

———————

Frequently though, no matter what we do, our past returns to haunt us. We can put the gun away, ease our way carefully through a ticklish situation, argue our way into an arrest, but for some of us there are moments when we too become instruments of violence. The ramifications of those moments are never easy.

Take Patrolman Judd and the purse snatcher.

Purse snatching seems like such a petty act. It's an impersonal transferal of liquid assets. Except that when it happened to this tiny black woman, she decided not to complete the transaction. She wouldn't let go and she yelled like hell. Her assailant, a man named Oscar Brown, beat her and left her bleeding on the sidewalk.

As Brown fled along Fox Street, an unmarked car driven by Patrolman Judd cut into his path. Brown pulled a .32 from his belt. He fired. Judd returned the fire with his police special .38 and killed Brown almost instantly. It was the first time in his career that Judd had ever killed a man.

An added edge to the tragedy was Judd's pride in his community work. He too was, black and for many years had worked in Harlem precincts where he earned a well-deserved reputation for his tough but humane treatment of offenders. Up to this moment, he had never used his weapon.

Later that evening, Oscar Brown's mother came to the Four-one to pick up her son's property. She had been there before; a long yellow sheet listed Brown's previous arrests in the precinct. As she waited, Judd walked by.

She smiled. "Patrolman Judd," she said, "don't you remember me?"

He hesitated. The face seemed familiar, but he wasn't sure. "It must be from Harlem, years ago," he said.

"Remember 4316 Lenox Avenue? The name is Sarah."

He remembered. "Why you're the sweet little thing that was always teasing me. Hey, I remember the day I helped deliver your first baby. Your daddy got me drunk and I had hell to pay with the sergeant." He basked in the recollection. "Things were pretty good on Lenox then," he said.

The woman's face broke into creases. She began to cry and Judd put his arms around her. "What's wrong, baby?"

"They've killed my baby, my little boy Oscar. They say he shot at a policeman."

Judd shuddered and pulled away. "Oscar Brown was your boy," he said.

She nodded.

"I'm sorry, Sarah," he said and walked away.

It took her nearly a minute to grasp his meaning and then she started screaming.

———————

It's six in the morning. It will be cool this day. The streets – hopefully – will be as clear. We park on the corner of Fox and Prospect and watch a coal truck as it jockeys into position, looking not unlike a large, anxious dog closing in on a hydrant. We watch it rise and spill its load down the chute.

Moe has Cora on his mind. I think that if she wasn't married the mush would be chasing her tail. Then I cancel that speculation. If there is one part of Moe's life that he's happy about, it's his family. He happens to like Cora. I let him prattle on. I am looking at Fox Street, in the morning. It's a different world.

Slowly, at first, the workers are on the street and heading downtown. Most of them are black and Puerto Rican, and their dignified bearing and smart dress belie their miserable surroundings. Moe and I play an irreverent game trying to figure out what jobs they are going to. Our final grades would probably stink. But it doesn't matter. They. probably stare at us and wonder who we are and where we came from.

Soon the coveralled men and the women in jeans head down to the Hunts Point Market to relieve the lobster shift. The kids follow, seeking train or bus on their way to school.

Early morning is the best time of day on this street. The warm light smoothes the jagged edges. Shadows disappear. Those people up and on the street seem to have a purpose; they seem to want to live. Later, the junkie, the mugger, will take control, but for these brief minutes Fox Street belongs to the people who really live there. Seeing them emerge each morning somehow makes my night seem worthwhile. I tell Moe to move and we drive over to Mushman's for some coffee.

6

DESPITE FREQUENT, unexpected, and often appalling intrusions, my daily tour at the Four-one assumed a certain, cruel rhythm. It began well before I left for work. Over coffee, I would feel myself growing tense. I knew I was about to leave safety and my body took every precaution against danger. After I kissed my wife good-bye and got in the car, my adrenalin would boost for the inevitable challenges; a lurking depression deepened as I contemplated the nature of those challenges.

After greeting the men at the desk, my first job was to read and initial the reports on the unusual incidents that occurred while I was off-duty. The reports gave me a total picture of the Four-one. I never knew whether to laugh or frown. This afternoon, Larry Bell, the lieutenant I relieved, walked over.

"The creeps are lousy shots in this precinct," he said. By now his voice was a Four-one voice, sympathetic tones of irony, laughter, and sorrow. When the men smiled you smiled. No sense shaking them up by pretending you didn't understand – everyone in the precinct understood.

"Last night there was a gun battle on the street and they killed an elderly lady sitting in her living room," Bell said. "She was reading a letter from her boy who's in Nam. Today they shot a kid who was playing basketball." Frowns filled the folder today.

We baked in the oven of our car as we rolled through the parched streets. Only the sun, strong and unrelenting, could clear the streets of this precinct. Moe searched the sidewalks for some shade where we could gulp our iced tea. It was a Sunday. The Fort would be quiet since many people were at "the Bronx Riviera," otherwise known as Orchard Beach. In reality, Orchard Beach was a gentle scallop of sand carved into the side of Long Island Sound. Since it could be reached by taking the subway and then the bus, it was popular with Bronx residents on warm days like this.

The only problem we faced, with a great deal of dread, was the end of such days. The hours at the beach were spent with family and friends and usually a case or two of beer, if not something stronger. Come evening, the families returned, rested, relaxed, very loose, and willing to continue an enjoyable time. A day in the sun also created potentially dangerous situations when the men and women who inhabited the Four-one returned and faced once more their real situation – garbage-strewn streets, decaying housing, low-paying jobs. It must have seemed to some of them that they were the victims of a monstrously cruel joke. Unable to turn the other cheek, they turned on one another and there we were, as usual, in the middle.

Moe got restless and suggested that now was the time to hit the hydrants. Every movie and TV show that dealt with ghetto life featured happy youngsters frolicking beneath sprays of water emitted by open fire hydrants. On the surface it seems so innocent; at worst, a natural impediment for cabs and buses. But open hydrants mean lower water pressure. And lower water pressure, particularly in an area prone to sudden fires, is a hazard.

But we knew the kids had to have a chance to cool off. So the city purchased sprinklers that emitted steady streams of cool water and still kept the pressure up. Usually, when we had the time, we looked for open hydrants and for "hydrant mothers." Once we spotted an open hydrant, we put the sprinkler cap on. Then we tried to find someone in the immediate vicinity who would watch and turn the hydrant off whenever the kids weren't using them. It might seem like a minor concern, but making sure the kids had a place to cool off, and with officialdom's approval, was important. On a hot summer night, nothing can anger a ghetto community more than the sight of some cop turning off a hydrant.

After we dealt with several hydrants, Moe remembered that he had promised to bring a patrolman named Cory some coffee. Cory was watching a DOA at an abandoned building on Longfellow Avenue near 165th Street. At first glance, I realized the building had been abandoned not out of neglect but fright.

The DOA was on the fifth floor. The stairs ended at the second floor. Since neither of us are slight, we proceeded gingerly to the fourth floor. After several calls, Cory came to the door and then managed to make his way down to us, using what remained of a banister.

Emergency service had been called, Cory told us. The medical examiner had also been there but he had been so pissed off about the stairs being out that he had left. "When I get the body down, I'll call him," Cory said.

I signed his memo book, Moe gave him the coffee, and we watched as he shinnied his way upstairs. Up there the draft was good and he had a fine view of the Penn Central yards below. As a scooter man, Cory spent many hours patrolling those yards in an effort to prevent looting.

Then things picked up. The Tactical Patrol Force deployed along the north side of the precinct as part of a special drive against street crime in that area. After we left, Patrolman Cory saw some activity in the yard. Seven men were breaking into a boxcar. He tried to raise Central, but discovered, to his disgust, that the batteries in his walkie-talkie were too weak. As he made his treacherous descent to the street, he cursed the attendant who checks out all the special equipment.

In retrospect, I made a mistake. Actually two mistakes. We surrounded a factory on Garrison Avenue where a burglary was supposed to be in progress. Foolishly, I gave my walkie-talkie to a sector car and told Moe to come in with me and help roust the thieves. At the time, I figured it was more important for the sector car to have the portable because there was a shortage of such radios. I reasoned that they were more likely to run into troubles.

As we started to enter the factory, Cory made it down to the street. All of a sudden, his radio started working. But Central told him there were no cars available. If I had asked Moe to stay by the radio or hadn't given up my portable radio we might have responded. However, I hadn't, and therefore we didn't. Cory precipitously decided to challenge the thieves alone. Before setting out, he wisely told Central where he was going. Patrolman Harry Harris, sitting in Sector John in front of the precinct house while his partner dropped off a 61 (crime report), made a mental note of the transmission.

Unaware that they had been spotted, the robbers placidly took stereo sets off the boxcar. Since Cory was alone, his approach went unnoticed. When he identified himself, the thieves were startled into submission.

Ordering them out of the car, he lined up the seven men and started to march them toward the control tower.

He made a nearly fatal mistake. His missed one of the thieves. As Cory walked by the open door, the man leaped on him. Together they sprawled on the ground. Cory's gun skittered across the tracks. There was no sound in the yard except for the panting and grunting of the men who struggled over the hard rocks of the roadbed. A couple of the others he had tried to arrest joined the fight while the rest fled. Cory rapped one of his assailants on the side of the head; the body collapsed. Then Cory rocked sideways as something hard slammed into his right shoulder. He knew he should feel pain, but there was nothing except the dust and the sweat and the effort to gulp down some more air.

After several moments, Cory managed to scream "10-13" into his radio along with his approximate location. It was a call that under any circumstance numbs most policemen. Translated, the call means "assist patrolman." In most instances the officer making the call has no time to blurt out the particulars; he could be shot, stomped, or stabbed. We hear the call and feel a fervor that frequently approaches hysteria. Nothing and no one stands in the way of responding officers. Some time, you know, it could be you calling in a 10-13. You pray others will respond as quickly to the call as you do.

I suppose we attach a still deeper significance to the 10-13. It is an electronic alert that authority is being challenged. It strengthens our feeling that policemen serve under unremitting siege conditions. Some segment of the population is always watching, probing for a weakness, committed to striking once that weakness is revealed. A 10-13 means the delicate balance between respect and fear on the one hand, and frustration, anger, has tilted. Convention and normalcy disappear, revealing a plot whose exact outcome is unclear, but which with experience, you realize will assume some tragic form. A 10-13 is the last cry in the night a policeman wants to hear.

While this action was going on, a man named Phil Gonzalez drove slowly north on Westchester Avenue. He turned right on Hoe. Gonzalez, at that moment, was a relatively happy man. The car he drove was stolen and the theft, as yet, went undetected. Already an arrangement had been made for him to meet a friend at a certain location. Together they would strip the car and sell the parts. It was good business for Phil, and he had done it a hundred times before.

So he relaxed slightly as he drove down Hoe. The heat had driven everyone outdoors. Adults sat drinking beer on the stoops or stood around sidewalk domino games. They lounged casually in the late afternoon shade watching the kids dash with unrestrained energy through the shooting water of open hydrants and through the moving traffic.

Gonzalez knew the area, felt comfortable in the area. He knew where the potholes were, he knew where the whores hung out, he knew where the social clubs were, where the cars sat double-parked along the curb. He also knew the ease with which thieves could jump into the car or simply walk up to an open window and stick up a man. So his eye roamed carefully, searching for the hidden dangers. When the little girl ran out from between two parked cars, he didn't see her. The sound of the fender hitting her body was like a grapefruit splitting open as it struck a hot sidewalk. She was dead instantly.

Veteran of the area that he was, Gonzalez knew what to expect. He leaped from his car, dove into the nearest tenement, and made for the roof. Those in the street also knew what to do. They split into teams and moved into tenements on either end of the block. Then they made their way across the rooftops and through the halls toward each other.

Sirens wailed in the distance. The crowd hesitated. Had a call about the accident already been made? The sirens' noise increased in volume only to diminish as they passed the intersection of Westchester Avenue and Hoe. They were chasing Cory's 10-13. One car, Sector King, decided that Cory was going to get all the help he needed and moved on the call that had come in about the accident on Hoe.

Cory put up a helluva fight. The thieves attacked him with fists, feet, their teeth, boards, rocks. They were like kids whose pleasant sidewalk game had been interrupted by an insensitive parent. Less concerned with escape, they seemed more anxious to revenge an unwanted intrusion upon well-conceived plans.

They had him on the ground when Sector John arrived. Seeing the number of men, Harris broadcast another 10-13 and moved in. Not far behind was Sergeant Bartow. Quickly the yard became a series of small brawls. Dust swirled, kicked up by dancing feet. There were some hoarse shouts, mostly as the men swung and grunted. One by one, the thieves were brought under control, handcuffed, and loaded into the patrol cars. All were dirty and tired and some suffered lacerations. Cory was hustled to Lincoln

Hospital where it was reported he would be ready for duty in a week.

The crowd from Hoe Avenue converged on Gonzalez. They wanted street justice. Various punishments were hoarsely suggested, but none found general favor. Then like something out of a B western came the cry, "Let's string him up." The crowd roared. It seemed like a good idea. A rope was offered from the trunk of a car, a noose tied, and several people threw the rope over a lamppost. Others, no doubt imbued with a pungent sense of irony, pushed the stolen car into position beneath the street light.

Gonzalez kicked and screamed as they dragged him to the car and pulled him up on the roof. In seconds they slipped the noose around his neck and then pushed the car out from under him. He dropped, dangled for a minute. Fortunately, the two men holding the rope weren't prepared for the force of his descent. They let go and Gonzalez fell, his neck burned and twisted so painfully he was unable to scream.

The crowd decided to make a second try. At that moment Sector King turned the corner onto Hoe. A patrolman named Lord sized up the situation immediately and put out a 10-13, while his partner, O'Hara, tried to make his way toward Gonzalez. They shoved O'Hara to the ground as the stolen car was pushed clear of Gonzalez's feet once more. He swung by his neck above the street as the mob cheered lustily. Lord reacted quickly. He pulled his revolver out and shot it several times into the air. The crowd held fast.

Other units arrived. Wielding nightsticks they fought their way toward the dangling man. The men holding the rope suddenly became nervous and let him go. Gonzalez fell to the street unconscious. In all the commotion, O'Hara picked up the trampled and forgotten body of the little girl and carried her to his patrol car. Apparently the mob's motive was really bloodlust, not vengeance.

By that time, Moe and I had been alerted and were on the way to the scene. A grinding rhythm, so ferocious that it seemed calculated, set in. Was everyone in the Four-one conspiring to make our lives hell? I told Moe that downtown they claimed 90 percent of all 10-13's were unfounded.

He laughed. "That's down there. This place is a different story. Most are for real."

A call came over from the TPF requesting a 10-85 (meet a car) at the northern edge of the precinct. There was no response, so I told Central that I would get a car up there as soon as possible. As I replaced the mike, I found myself thinking, "Fat chance."

"Ten-thirteen on the street, Bryant Avenue and 172nd Street," came over the radio. That was just south of Tremont Avenue and Boston Road. No chance of any assistance. Have to hope for the best. This was one of those times when I felt like wrenching the radio from its brackets and flinging it out the window.

"That's number three," Moe said perfunctorily.

"Let's hit Hoe first," I told him.

As we turned into Hoe, only Sector King remained. The crowd was gone, slipped like wraiths into the dozens of doorways and alleys along the street. The screams of only minutes ago weren't even an echo now. Lord and O'Hara put Gonzalez into the back seat of their car, propping his comatose body against that of the little girl. Without a word – what could be said? – the two men got in and sped toward Lincoln Hospital.

Like a swelling tide, the crowd came back again, still excited, still looking for action. We saw it coming but we couldn't stop it. They wanted the stolen car. Quickly flames enveloped it. The mindlessness of it all stunned me. As we drove away my head groped for other items, other incidents, less barbaric, easier to cope with. But in the Four-one, that's a prayer never answered.

As we moved on the Bryant Avenue call, Moe told me that sometimes there was a big crap game near that location. "Maybe someone tried to take the game," he suggested. I preferred to wait.

It turned out someone did take the game. Twelve players were lined up against a wall as the cash was collected. Then the robbers opened fire with shotguns. When they split, those players that could move followed them. When we got there only the three most seriously wounded were still at the scene.

A TPF car had arrived just in time to see a blue Chevy with four men fleeing from the scene. They called in a 10-13. The radio crackled. Sector Peter started a chase down Boston Road, but none of our cars were in a position to intercept and the men escaped.

My mind reeled, splintered by calls that never ceased. I tried to sort it all out. No single stimulus made any sense, and since I had to solve each stimulus, some order must be fashioned between all of them. I had to dominate events, not succumb to them.

Sector King drove up and reported that Gonzalez was still alive. Okay, step one. "Get over and check the car," I told them. "And get on the horn and tell AIS (Accident Investigation Squad) to do their thing if the block is quiet enough. Better get the detectives on it. We might still have a homicide on our hands."

Affirmative action, that was what we needed. I turned to another car and told them to straighten out the crap game robbery. "Let's find out what happened now," I said sternly. "I don't want to hear about it next week." The men nodded solemnly.

Then Moe leaned out the window of our car. "Hey, Lou," he called sweetly, "another 10-13." I cursed and felt like kicking something.

"Anything else we missed?" I asked Moe when I got back in the car. Only later would Moe admit that he said "I don't think so" under his breath. In the meantime I sat and worried in the hot patrol car and soaked in my sweat and consternation.

The 10-13 came from Mineford Place. Two TPF foot patrolmen had arrested four gang members for assaulting a storekeeper. Since no units could respond immediately, they hailed a gypsy cab.

It was a dark and narrow street, and the crowd that gathered sensed the officers' vulnerability. They pressed in. They met drawn clubs. It seemed as if the air had taken on the ugly, turgid smell of blood.

As the units responded, ash cans, bricks, and bottles were hurled at them from the roofs. Two men were hit and crumpled to the ground almost immediately. One suffered a shoulder wound; the other lay amid the cans and bottles and torn grocery bags, moaning and holding his head, which was covered with blood. Within minutes, the street became a sea of broken glass. The sound of play, the talk of neighbors were replaced by the sharp reports of broken bottles and breaking windows.

First we responded with revolvers, raking the tops of tenements. We didn't fool around. Two of ours were in there and we meant to get them back. We stormed through the crowd, beating back anyone that stood in our way. The men had been badly beaten but were still conscious. Once they sensed our mood, the crowd backed off to nurse its own bruised shins and bloodied heads. The TPF pursued the escaped prisoners. They managed to recapture two of the four freed by the crowd.

Some calm came to the area and with it another 10-13. It seemed that no matter where we turned, where we moved, some implacable foe followed. In this instance, a resident had shot another resident. Only his friends didn't feel this warranted an arrest. As we rushed to the scene I shook my head. Five 10-13's. I couldn't believe it.

Moe was in an ugly mood. His injury at the earlier brawl still troubled him. But the series of events, one compounding the other, and all so senseless, so needless, the injuries of seven men, all had depleted what goodwill he felt toward the residents of Fort Apache. Which put me in a downer. Moe is the most easygoing of men, so when he's depressed there has to be a particularly good reason for it. We drove to our fifth 10-13 in silence.

Four cars flamed into the night when we arrived. By now it was twilight; men became eerie shadows as they stumbled beneath the uncertain glare of the street lights. Debris streamed down from the roofs, but by now this was almost commonplace, even expected. We recognized fellow officers by the blue of their helmets that gleamed like steel robins' eggs in the night. We formed a wedge and pushed our way to the cops and their prisoner. Then, as usual, we retreated, but in good order. The fire department wanted no part of this street that night, so the cars were left to burn themselves out.

I felt exhausted and depressed. We would go into a street, achieve whatever our limited goal was, absorb some wounds and bruises, bleed a bit, and then retreat. A chaotic darkness would then follow our departure and all we could do was listen for the next 10-13. For the first time, the Four-one's savage rhythm struck me. No matter its chords or its counterpoint, violence hit us and the people again and again and again.

And then I wondered how the men could continue to cope. How much energy can a man expend on vain effort before he says, "Fuck this." Like a wanderer in a snowstorm who can no longer see his hands in front of him and finally succumbs to the cold. At such a moment home, for us, was at its most alluring.

As abruptly as they began, the 10-13's stopped. Moe and I hustled back to the station house where I spent the next hour or so cleaning up the details and preparing a couple of 49's (unusual reports). Then we grabbed a cup of coffee. We drove back to the water's edge where we could sip in peace. The cool air, the play of lights on the bay, and the grace of those distant airliners helped soothe us.

We talked about the probability of five 10-13's within that span of time. No logical or even mystical explanation appeared. It wasn't the first or the fifteenth of the month – the days the welfare checks arrive. This might seem like prejudice, but those are the nights the booze flows, and if either of those dates fall on a Friday, you can expect the worst. You can look it up.

And then we checked the moon but it still had two weeks to go before reaching its full phase.

The Fort fell silent as we licked our wounds. We drove slowly through the suddenly quiet streets. Our night wasn't over though. Suddenly, a call came from a Four-three portable unit. "It's heading south on Bruckner Boulevard toward the Four-one."

Then silence.

"What's the color and make?" asked a Four-one car.

Silence.

Then, "It looks like it's going into the Four-one."

What was it, Godzilla? King Kong? Mayor Lindsay's next budget? Again our unit asked for a description. No answer came.

The Four-three man was now screaming, "He's exiting into the Four-one."

Several of our units moved nearer to the highway. They called for a description. Still silence. Moe moved into a good position at the intersection of Hunts Point Avenue and Bruckner Boulevard.

A voice drifted over the radio, hesitant, decidedly sheepish. "It's a green and white Plymouth, Central."

Four-one Sector King's voice didn't even betray a smile. "We're on their tail, Central," they advised and then added, "Central, would you please ask that pursuing Four-three car if the vehicle in question has a dome light on the roof?

A green and white Plymouth quickly flashed by our position. Sector King, siren blasting, was right behind. We joined the chase. We finally pulled the car over on Tiffany Street. Two red-faced men from the Four-three eventually showed up to retrieve their car.

The story was not willingly told. Two officers had stopped at a deli, at the corner of Castle Hill Avenue and Bruckner Boulevard. While they were inside ordering a sandwich, along comes this drunk who needs a ride home. He spots a car, its engine running, and decides that he is not put off by its color scheme, its run-down interior, or its special options. He takes off in this funny-looking car and is then chased by other funny-looking cars. Finally he stops to find out what it's all about. We let the man stumble on his way home. I wondered if his friends would believe the story – or if he would even remember it at all.

Eventually, the two officers got their car back. But not before Moe and I gleefully monitored them saying, "Just get it back." Then, "Too bad you didn't get the thief." We laughed, but we also knew they were lucky. They would have faced charges if any formal report had been filed. It wasn't and two cops learned to be a little more careful with their vehicle.

Finally I hauled my weary backside home. A scotch and a shower and I was shortly snoozing comfortably. Then the phone rang. It was Moe. He was in Happy's on Westchester Avenue.

"Hey, Lou," he said.

"Wha?"

"Want to know what we forgot?"

"Wha?" Suddenly I sat up, my mind back in the South Bronx. "What the hell time is it? Forgot?"

"The stiff."

"What stiff?"

"Cory's stiff – the DOA on Longfellow."

"Oh. shit." I remembered. When Cory went to roust those thieves, he left a DOA on the fifth floor of that building. I told Moe to call the precinct. I wasn't going to chase down there after it. I thought I heard Moe laugh as he hung up but I wasn't sure. I slowly rocked myself back to sleep.

7

WHEN I WOKE UP the next morning, I felt as if I had a hangover. My eyes ached, my mouth felt dry. I lay still, expecting that any moment the silence would be shattered by the static of the radio and the call "10-13." The image, I realize, is melodramatic, but then I felt like hell, and when you feel like hell, being dramatic becomes an ineluctable quality. My wife moved quietly in the kitchen. I knew I would have to return to the Fort. That was all part of the give-and-take, the push-and-shove. I wanted more sleep although I realized I wouldn't know what to do with it.

Over coffee, I sketched the previous night's occurrences to my wife. It seemed that I prefaced every item with the phrase "You're not going to believe this but..." No matter how outlandish my account, I felt she did try to understand. And it wasn't always easy to describe how close I sometimes got to the depravity, the desperation. How quickly and unobtrusively the Four-one became a part of our lives. She worried but tried not to show it. Hand-wringing wasn't part of her personality.

So my mind swung back to the Fort. By that I mean the station house, the center, where all the shit is directed. While I sat in that bright kitchen in Co-op City, my mind grubbed among the trash on Simpson Street. Many mornings I would brood on what I had seen and heard and felt in the Fort.

Take the night the Indian was pulled into the station house. Fifty years old. Short, stocky, with a

Mohawk haircut. He turned out to be a full-blooded Seminole. Everyone smiled – after all, this is Fort Apache; nothing should surprise us. The presence of an Indian was no more incongruous than, say, if the QE II decided to tie up at the mouth of Bronx River. If the mouth of the Bronx River could ever be found.

He said his name was Jim. He was from Florida and he rode the rails starting in Florida and ending up in the Hunts Point Market.

"I wanted to see the country," he explained. "It is my country." I saw no argument in that. He said that he decided to "walk to the city."

At the corner of Westchester Avenue and Southern Boulevard, two guys jumped him. That's when the cops arrived. On the surface his explanation seemed plausible, but I wanted to know more.

I asked Bill Ruth what happened. "He's right," Ruth said. "A couple of guys tried to hustle him. They got away. Then he went after everyone in sight. We had to get him off the street; he must have slugged ten people."

"Did you have any complainants?" He shook his head. "The only reason we brought him in was that we thought he was a little crazy," Ruth said.

At that point, Jim, who was listening to the report, went berserk. He struggled violently to get out of the cuffs. "I'm not crazy," he screamed. "I'm not crazy." It took us a couple of minutes to calm him down. Finally I had him put in the cage, a makeshift cell on the main floor where prisoners are kept for further deposition.

For a moment, I was back in P.S. 68. I could hear my seventh grade teacher, Mrs. Bush, telling the class in 1947, "When you get old enough to vote, do something for the Indians." I'm sure she had something else in mind, but I couldn't see any point in hanging on to him. He was his own man; he wasn't looking for trouble. Perhaps the ways of the city baffled him. After he calmed down, a car took him back to the market. There, the men put him on a truck heading south. The Fort, I knew by then, existed for more than a collection of policemen.

That night, the TPF assigned a group of new men to work the six-to-two shift. They stood sharp and tall. The platoon commander conducted his inspection with unusual sharpness. Then, barely breaking stride, they marched out the front door.

As they hit the street, the bugle blared at them. "Da-da-dah. Da-da-dah . . ." Taps wafted through the air. The TPF stopped. Across the street, on the parapet of a tenement roof, stood a man wearing what looked like a moth-eaten Ike jacket and wrinkled fatigues. His silhouette swooped in mock salute. Then once again he raised his bugle.

Sergeant Phil Grimes told the men, "It's okay; he's on our side."

The man's name was Juan Chicano and he was a World War I veteran. When he was so moved, he greeted the shift change with this stirring salute. As the TPF started for their posts I heard one man say, "Now I know what they mean about this place. You have to see it to believe it." He didn't even know half the story.

Moe and I and a couple of guys were talking about the Knapp Commission, which had stirred great confusion and consternation among the men. On the one hand, most agreed that the corruption must be rooted out. On the other, they felt that the use of television and publicity demeaned them all, lessened their stature, made their jobs more difficult. We argued for several minutes before the dogs showed up.

Earlier an elderly couple had reported an attack by wild dogs. This looked like the same pack. We scrambled into the vestibule. I told the TS operator to call the ASPCA. As we stood in the doorway, the dogs approached but did not pursue us.

We thought we could shoo them off when a truck from the storehouse pulled up. The driver got out and walked toward us. Moe opened the door. "Stay away from those damn dogs," he yelled. "The heat's got them." The driver laughed.

"You brave Fort Apache heroes afraid of a few dogs," he said. He strolled leisurely up the steps. "You guys can at least sign for a package." I signed for it.

"Fort Apache." He murmured the words sarcastically as he walked back to the truck.

As he finished the third syllable, a rangy shepherd raced over and sunk his teeth deeply into the driver's thigh. Actually, the action took place more slowly than that, although we remained frozen, stunned by the suddenness and justice of the act. First the man turned his back to the dogs. He made his remarks. The shepherd lunged, teeth exposed. For perhaps a tenth of a second, the driver realized his fate; he tried to swing out of the way. The dog reached him, fabric tore, teeth punctured flesh, and the man screamed.

"Get the fuckin' thing off me," he yelled.

Joe Pitts ran out with his blackjack. I knew Pitts was quick but not that quick. While man and dog squirmed on the ground, Pitts leaned over and administered two sharp blows to the dog's head.

The driver suffered a bad bite. He also suffered from a not-so-curious lack of sympathy. In fact some of us were probably rooting for the dog.

"Stupid bastard," Pitts said. "The number one rule around here is to always protect your ass. Never underestimate an opponent, not even a dog."

Then Pitts threw some salt on the wound. "Where the hell did you learn to be a cop – in Scarsdale?" he said. The man groaned.

One night, someone burglarized the Fort during a late tour. I laughed. But the men working inside the house that night couldn't even smile.

Then a man suggested, "Maybe we should hire Burns guards." That broke the tension a little bit.

I asked the sergeant what the hell happened. Was anybody crapped out? I wanted to know.

"No, everything was routine," he said. Which meant hell broke loose about 90 percent of the time. "We were going all night," he said. "I can't understand it."

Whatever jokes could have been milked from the situation soon evaporated when I found out what had been taken. Entering through an old coal chute, the burglars broke into PAL lockers and desks taking athletic and office equipment. Alone, the act would have been enough. But before leaving the thieves defecated on the floor and used old precinct marching flags to wipe themselves. This act went beyond mere sickness. We could think of no motive. Once again, the neighborhood had attacked itself.

We came to view the Fort as an island in the trash. Curiously, the Fort lent us a feeling of immortality. Drive down Simpson Street and there squatted that Neo-Florentine palace squinting through iron bars at the grimy world outside. Enter it and you and the others on that shift braced yourselves against the world. You sensed, somehow, you would endure. Someone else would always get it, someone else would go over the wall or around the bend. It was always someone else, the poor bastard.

Then moments came when the outside world intruded. Reacting properly, like putting on your best suit in a hurry, became difficult. Once upon a time, even the Police Commissioner visited us.

The Fort was hopping. The temperature was 98 degrees in the street, and it was at least 108 in the station house. The TS operator called to me, "Hey, Lou, Four-five on the phone."

"Okay, I'll pick it up at the 124 desk."

"Lieutenant Walker here. What can I do for ya."

"Hey, Lou, the P.C.'s on his way to the Four-one," an excited voice said.

"Great, how long do I have?" I asked.

"He left here a couple of minutes ago. He wants to catch the midnight platoon at the Four-one."

"A little pep talk, huh? The men will love it," I said.

I alerted Sergeant Jim Fennel on the desk and slipped to my basement retreat to take off my savers. Savers are old uniforms which are usually worn on late tours – they save your good uniforms.

The Police Commissioner's black, air-conditioned Mercury stopped in front of the station house. A small, almost ghostlike figure emerged and nervously looked around. His balding, egg-shaped head reinforced his intellectual image. Somehow, he didn't look like a cop.

The officer on station-house security, the Polack, was now standing in the street, looking around for a parking spot for the P.C.'s car. There weren't any. He gave the Commissioner a sloppy salute. The P.C. walked stiffly up the front steps of the Fort. He didn't walk like a cop.

The Polack shrugged and said to the chauffeur, "You gotta move it. There're no spots left. I have to keep the block open."

The chauffeur frowned, started to get out of his car, then changed his mind and said, "You can't get one of these cars out of here?"

"Which one do you suggest?" the Polack coldly asked.

"What about the black Chevy?"

"You must be kidding. That's Lieutenant Walker's. I have to live with him."

"Fuckin' place," the chauffeur yelled and shot down the street burning rubber.

The Polack clapped his hands and smiled.

Sergeant Fennel was very busy at the desk and didn't see the Commissioner enter. The P.C. stopped, anticipating some recognition, but nobody called "Attention." Rosa, at the reception desk, said, "Can I help you, mister?" The Commissioner, still looking serious, responded by shaking his head and moved toward the cigar-puffing sergeant. A street mutt ran barking from behind the desk making the P.C. change course. Several officers in casual conversation in the sitting room spotted the Commissioner. One officer split from the group and moved toward Rosa as the rest started to laugh.

Patrolman Mike DePola on a confiscated minibike came roaring up the steps of the Fort and burst into the muster room. The noise was deafening. Only now did Sergeant Fennel look up and yell, "Get off that goddamn thing." Seeing the P.C. he yelled, "Attention" and pressed the buzzer for the men to fall in. Jim saw Rosa adjusting her sweater. He knew what she planned to do. He ran past the P.C. toward Rosa saying, "Excuse me a second, Commissioner."

"Rosa, that's the P.C., don't do it. He'll have my ass, *comprende*?" Jim said.

"Oh, Joe told me him a new lieutenant," Rosa said. Through all this the serious expression on the P.C.'s face never changed.

Sergeant Savage had the men lined up as the Commissioner entered the sitting room. I came flying up the stairs from my hole in the basement with my best uniform on. Sergeant Fennel stopped me saying, "He's here already, in the sitting room. I don't think your new uniform is going to help any."

"Tell me later. I better get in there," I said.

The P.C. nodded to me as I moved alongside the sergeant. I smiled saying softly, "Hello, Commissioner, happy to have you." He nodded again.

Sergeant Savage finished calling the roll and said, "Commissioner."

The Commissioner stepped forward to speak. I looked at the platoon. They had the death mask on and were looking past him.

They're a tough audience, I thought to myself.

"I came here tonight to tell you that I think you are doing a great job. I know that you have a difficult assignment..." The speech lasted five minutes. The Commissioner said what the men had expected. It was rah-rah number two. When he finished the Commissioner shook my hand saying, "You're doing a great job, keep it up," and left. The men came to life.

"Why the hell did he come here? He don't even talk like a cop," Tom Roark said.

"Yeah, we're getting stomped, stabbed, and shot and all he's worrying about is corruption. Where're his fuckin' priorities?" Joe Pitts added.

"He's got balls coming here," another officer said.

Sergeant Savage turned to me. "It's true, you have to admit it, the guy's got balls to face these guys," he said.

In a sense the Commissioner was an outsider, while we were all insiders. He must have sensed the gap between us, even the hostility some of us felt for the downtown brass who could tour the city in a chauffeur-driven car. Still he faced us and saluted and then turned and left.

The Commissioner walked past the smiling Rosa into the street. His annoyed chauffeur was halfway through his seventeenth trip around the block at the time. The Commissioner stood on the steps absorbing the sights, sounds, and smells of Simpson Street. "Nice place to visit, huh, boss," the Polack offered.

The Commissioner, picking up the connotation, said, "We have to make the entire city a nice place to

115

visit." The Mercury pulled up. "Keep up the good work, Officer," he said as he hurried to his car. It sped off .

"Keep up the good work," the Polack said out loud.

"What the hell did he mean by that?"

Moe and I were out checking factories for burglars. On our way back, we spotted a car parked in a space and at a time when cars weren't normally there. He shined his flashlight into the car.

"Only a couple of lovers going at it." he said nonchalantly over his shoulder. Moe, I knew, would be content to let them go. My concern was prostitution and the crime that often accompanies this vice.

"Tell them to get out of here I said. "Tell them we'll be back in five minutes."

"Did you hear the lieutenant?" Moe asked.

Back came a barely audible answer, "Yeah."

"Sorry, buddy," Moe said. "I hope you didn't lose it."

We drove off. Moe laughed.

"He lost it all right. Did ya see the look on his face?"

Moe settled down somewhat. "Still, that's a shitty thing to do to a guy," he said.

I pondered my own reasons. Like a lot of cops I tend to feel that it isn't our job to legislate morality unless immoral acts hurt someone, especially children. But I also ascribed to certain standards of taste and this scene violated them, and the law.

"I wonder why the stupid bastard doesn't go to a motel."

"Too poor probably," Moe said.

A couple of hours later, I saw the same guy come into the station house. He didn't see me as he went to the 124 desk. He left several minutes later and I went over.

"What did that guy want?" I asked.

"He reported a burglary. Someone stole his poor box."

"His poor box?" I still had a streak of naiveté running through me. The Four-one continually surprised me; I sniffed like a stray dog along its curb, always encountering some new, surprising scent. "Who the hell is he?" My innocent question drew guilty grins, venal chuckles.

"That was the Reverend Riley," said one officer. "You've heard of him. He has the parish over at St.——. He's the anti-war minister. You know, make love not war."

I choked back a laugh. Later, I told Moe about my discovery. "I'd rather see them that way," he said, "than the other way." For me, morality had wiggled its hip in yet another fashion. Would I ever adapt?

*

The captain wanted to fix up the lounge for the men. One of the PBA delegates, an officer named Jack Binn, offered an old pool table he had at home. Several men went over to his house with a truck and brought it back. They set it up in the lounge. Things were shaping up.

The next morning, Moe and I wandered into the lounge for a game of eight-ball. Moe said he would rack up the balls while I chalked the tips of the cues.

Both of us suffered the same sensation. Like Alice, we had suddenly grown too big for the world. We looked again. No, the world had gotten too small. Someone had sawed the legs off the pool table.

One night as we approached the station house, a small, lithe man hurtled out the door. As he crossed in front of us, our headlights caught the reflection of metal hanging from his wrist. A second later, more light. The barrel of a Smith and Wesson belched light, cracked sharply. The .38 flashed six times. Zero. Men emerged, shouting that a homicide suspect had escaped. The detective chasing the man disappeared into an alley after him. Moe gunned the car down Simpson then pulled a right on Fox Street.

"I don't see anything," I said.

"Neither do I," he said.

What we didn't know was that the two men had already passed us. Moe called a 10-85 with three cars and we surrounded the block. We searched the area diligently but with little success.

A sector car pulled up to the curb. "What are you guys doing?" the driver asked.

"Looking for the escaped prisoner." I was tempted to say blueberries but they might have believed that.

They still looked incredulous. "The guy's been in the house for the last 25 minutes." one said. I moaned. Was this another classic example of detective-patrol cooperation?

Moe called it survival. "You'll never hear anything about a prisoner on the radio. It's an automatic complaint to lose a prisoner. Most guys would rather lose a prisoner for a couple of hours than get a complaint. We know we'll get them back before the night's over – where the hell do they have to go?" It was something to think about.

That same night, Patrolman Black Jack Ferris learned that a gun exchange was scheduled. It could be that one gang had shotguns, the other pistols. Although the scale was small, we faced a steady arms trade. The result of such exchanges was usually death. Feuding nations buy jets and missiles; here it's Saturday Night Specials.

We covered a minipark at Bryant Avenue and 167th Street. The two anti-crime men, disguised as bums, walked the perimeter of the area. As the night wore on, the park filled with youths. A little after 10 P.M. one of the officers spotted one man handing a package to another. They stopped the recipient as he hurried from the park. Someone yelled, "The pigs, they got Tony!" A brawl erupted as gang members tried to rescue their friend. A 10-13 went out.

Ten cars answered the call. Ferris's partner, a man named Joe Cairo, was slightly injured. The youth named Tony remained in custody. I should have known what was going to happen.

An hour later a mob closed in on the Fort. They seemed determined to rescue Tony. We followed our normal defense procedures. The door was slammed shut, the men camped by the windows. "Here we go again," the Polack yelled as we moved into position.

These attacks had become so common that the men moved almost casually to their posts. I stood there and ran over a mental checklist: lights out, roof covered, and barriers at door, and then I had the TS make the routine call to Central. "We are under attack," the operator said. "Better send a few cars." He paused. "And an ambulance too."

"Ten-four, Four-one base," was the response. Central sounded bored.

The crowd was mostly young; many carried bricks, bats, and rocks. First they launched a missile assault. Anything at hand, bottles, stones, garbage cans were hurled at the Fort. It survived. Inside, we sat out the initial assault. Six men moved next to Moe and the Polack at the front door. The Polack peeked out. "They've backed off. Maybe they're out of ammo," he said.

"See any guns?" A newly assigned officer asked the question. We didn't answer. He'd know the answer soon enough.

My mind wavered between standing pat or meeting them on the street. One action offered minimal injury; the other might lead to a prolonged siege and possibly an expansion of violence to other blocks. I hoped I sounded a lot more confident than I felt.

"Okay," I said in my best John Wayne tone of voice.

"We'll meet them in the street. They don't seem that organized. Remember, break them into small groups." Inside, I was telling myself I really didn't know what the hell was on out there.

Time favored us. In a few minutes, radio cars would surround the area. The thought hit me. Wait for their arrival. No, deal with the situation now. It's the kind of moment that makes you sweat and shake a little. Then the next morning, your wife takes one look at your shirt and wants to know why the hell the collar is so dirty.

I grabbed a megaphone and started talking. "There's no point to this," I said. I might as well have spoken through a hollow beer can. My voice tumbled across the street and got lost in the alleyways and air-shafts. "Look, Tony had a loaded gun on him. He'll get his day in court tomorrow." The phrase "day in court" echoed with an empty ping. I believed it. Did they? They saw the courts and the judicial system as a place where men were swallowed whole, caught in a sea of law books and law, hostile police and stern judges. We saw the system as being antiquated, over-worked, and inefficient, a place where an accused felon's "day" might be only a matter of minutes before he was back out on the streets again. "You know as well as I do," I screamed, "that he'll be out in the morning." True, oh, so true.

"Bull-sheet man," came the answer. "We want our man now, you hear that, motherfucker." That from a man called Bomber. I made a mental note to get him first when everything broke loose, which it did almost immediately.

Nine of us, clasping nightsticks, ringed the steps when the mob charged. I pounced on the Bomber put-ting him out of action with a stomach blow. The score was evened when the Polack sank to his knees, clutching his groin. Bats and pipes and sticks swirled through the air. After several seconds, both sides went head-hunting, seeking the weakest, the most vulner-able of the opposition. Several of the youths fell, holding bleeding heads or grabbing at severely bruised shoulders. Battered and bloodied officers were dragged back in the house. We barely held our own.

Then sirens were heard at both ends of Simpson Street. The mob split, its temporary cohesiveness lost

121

with the approach of forces from the rear. Still, it took us another half an hour to clear the block. Four men were injured; three of them with head wounds. I was pissed but the men accepted their injuries calmly. Why, I asked, should anyone accept this type of senseless attack? They agreed with the nouns and the adjectives but shrugged off the verb as meaningless. It was unavoidable; an inextricable part of the social fabric of the area. I was still pissed.

The Polack tried to help. "Maybe we should have waited longer," he said.

"Thanks a lot, you bastard," I said.

The bells and the bongos were still welcoming in the new year when we had our first homicide. I picked up the phone and dialed the medical examiner's office. Before I could speak, a voice said, "You're calling from the Four-one, right."

"Yeah," I said. I could hear voices and some laughter in the background.

Finally the voice came back on, "Betting on the Four-one is like betting on the old Yankees – they always came through. Second year in a row I made money on the Four-one, thanks."

He took the message and hung up. I should have laughed but I felt like tearing the phone out of the wall. Was that all we were, a number in a pool? I hoped the bastard went out to celebrate his good fortune with a T-bone steak and choked on it.

8

CAPTAIN RYAN was transferred. The Police Commissioner was very concerned about the state of the 41st Precinct. Headquarters called it "the Fort Apache syndrome." Chief Klein of the Inspections Division was directed to debrief Captain Ryan to determine what could be done about the situation in the Four-one. Captain Ryan defined the Fort Apache syndrome as the attitude of the men that "We're in the worst place on earth; we work harder than anyone in the Police Department; no one cares about us or our problems so therefore we are entitled to do as we please because the normal rules don't apply to us."

It is obvious that a modem urban police department cannot tolerate such an attitude. But where does the blame lie? Did the policemen assigned to this precinct make it the most crime-ridden area in the history of civilization? Were many undesirables transferred into the Four-one from other precincts? Were they responsible for the endemic drug culture?

The questions go on and on. On top of all this, they were, and still are the most shot-at group of men in this supposedly civilized country. Is it any wonder that they improvised and made their own rules?

The men of the Four-one have been tested and retested in many ways, and most have survived. But we have also had our casualties. I speak here not of casualties of the body, but casualties of the mind and soul. For too many years the Department was unconcerned or unaware of the price many of these men were paying. On the day Chief Klein interviewed Captain Ryan, 35 percent of the police officers in the Four-one had already requested a transfer. After I had one year in the Four-one, there were only two patrol supervisors who had been there for the entire year; myself and Sergeant Saverin. During that first year I saw approximately seventy superiors arrive and leave. The patrolmen lacked this maneuverability. They had to remain, adjust, and, hopefully, survive. Most did, but there were casualties.

The night was cool. The patrol car, its windows cracked slightly to prevent carbon monoxide poisoning, rolled up to the traffic light. The small figure in the recorder's seat saw something that frightened him. His face contorted with fear, he drew his service revolver, and fired once. He fired again and screamed, "They're all over the floor, they're all over the floor, they're going to get us."

The operator of the patrol car, at first frightened, looked at the floor of the car and saw nothing. There was nothing there. He said calmly, "It's okay, put the gun away."

The small uncertain figure said, "Are you sure? They might come back. Are you sure?"

"It's okay, it's okay," the response came. The small figure placed the revolver back into his holster, as the vehicle made a U-turn and headed toward the station house.

Police officer Trusk was a small, young, and intense officer who had been in the precinct for about two years. Trusk had spent two years in a quiet precinct and done well. He was ready for bigger things. During his first two months in the Four-one he seemed to handle his jobs well. He was shot at once but it didn't seem to faze him. The workload was heavy and the jobs difficult. One night he was handling a stabbing on the street and a large, boisterous crowd gathered. He called a 10-13. The responding units found a large crowd but no serious problems. Two nights later Trusk called a 10-13 at a family fight; his partner called it off. The men started to wonder about him.

Pains in the stomach caused Trusk to report sick several times. A GI series found nothing wrong. His doctor advised that it was a nervous stomach. Trusk began to carry a little brown medicine bottle around with him; it was filled several times each tour by bartenders in his sector. Within eight months he had a serious drinking problem. Tough jobs directed to his car went unanswered. He picked up the easy jobs and milked them. The sergeants knew what he was doing and got on his back. He received a couple of command disciplines for minor infractions.

His mother couldn't understand what was happening to him. He became remote at home. When questioned, he became hostile. With a girlfriend in the precinct, he now spent more time away from home. A social drinker in the past, he had quickly degenerated into an alcoholic. He was hospitalized with a serious wound when his girlfriend hit him with a bat during an argument.

Emerging from the hospital, he continued his precinct syndrome: drinking and girls. His work habits and health deteriorated together. A bleeding ulcer sidelined him for a short time. It was soon after his return to work following the ulcer problem, that he was attacked by the "creatures" on the floor of the radio car.

He was retired from the force on a disability and has been in and out of mental hospitals ever since.

*

Patrolman Stock was a great cop – aggressive, smart, and courageous. A happily married suburbanite, he had three children. Having spent the whole of his ten years as a policeman in the Four-one, he had seen everything; the mangled bodies, the vice, the wanton brutality, the hostility. In spite of all this, he, like most of the officers, was well adjusted. Always smiling with a good word for all, that was Stock. He had many friends among the bodega owners and residents on his post. One of the first to object to blanket indictments of the people in the area, he could cite many instances where the people on his post had saved his life.

One day Stock approached me and said casually, "I think I've had enough of the Four-one. It's been fun but I think I'm ready for something else." I signed his UF 57 (request for transfer). It wasn't refused, but he was told that he would have to wait. He waited and waited. Stock felt this was an injustice and showed his anger. The smile disappeared from his round face, the kind words ceased. This was not the Stock I knew. I was concerned. I mentioned it to the boss; he shrugged saying, "What the hell can I do? I can't take everyone off patrol. The station house looks like a psychiatric ward already."

A week later the windshield of Stock's private car was smashed, the battery was stolen, and the tires slashed. Stock's face grew tense, furrows creased his forehead. That night he dragged a bloodied prisoner into the station house. The prisoner, a car thief, had taken a swing at Stock in an effort to escape. Stock responded defensively but got carried away. I called him into a side office. He looked like he was about to cry. "Get me out of here before I kill someone," he blurted out. I calmed him down and promised to do my best to get him out. The next day was my regular day off but I came in to see the C.O. about Stock. He assigned Stock to an inside job, although we were already over-crowded with officers we were afraid to put on the street. It took several months but the transfer finally came through. Stock was sent to a "slow" precinct in Queens. Thirteen months later he made detective, the result of outstanding work. One had been saved.

Marital problems are not unusual for many policemen. Some wives can't adjust to the disruptive schedule, the absences on holidays, the long nights alone, the fear when the phone rings late at night, and, most of all, the changes that may take place in a young man learning the police trade. He may curse more, start drinking or stay out more. His feelings may harden in a self-defensive response to daily stimuli. He may become cynical or may be frightened by the job. There are many significant and very small ways in which a man may change when exposed to places like the Four-one. Many rookie officers arrive here with absolutely no understanding of the culture of the ghetto. Some are frightened by it and some overcompensate and try to become part of it. Luckily, most adjust fairly well within a year or so. It is from the first two groups that most of the problems arise. Because of the fear or the overcompensation, their conduct changes. Their wives are the first to suffer.

One young officer in our area had a serious problem at home. He loved his wife but was at a loss to solve their deteriorating relationship. Discovering that she had taken a lover, he fell apart. He drove his vehicle to a quiet spot on Hunts Point Avenue to think things over. He finally found a solution. Placing his .38 caliber revolver to his mouth, he blew his brains out.

Another officer with family problems became a heavy drinker. After six years in the Four-one, he was an alcoholic. He blamed the precinct for his problems but was unable to get out. The people on the street quickly learned to avoid him. A surly word, an improper glance, or an annoying situation directed to him meant that someone was going to catch a fist. He was removed from the street and given an inside job. His wife divorced him. When I left the Four-one, he was still there, brooding and drinking.

Another drinker with marital problems was standing on a corner. For some unknown reason, he fired at a gypsy cab as it passed. The driver of the gypsy cab couldn't believe it, so he circled the block. Passing the officer for the second time, he was shot at again. This time, using a little more common sense, the driver came into the precinct. This officer's problems were a little more involved and he is still undergoing psychiatric treatment. A final disposition of his case is still pending.

In the Four-one, even the combat-seasoned fall prey to the effects of battle. Take the case of Bill Korr. A young, handsome, and sincere officer, Korr was happily married. His record in the Four-one had been outstanding. He had been shot in the stomach a couple of years earlier coming to the aid of another officer. I had little doubt that he would eventually make detective.

It was about 1:45 A.M. when a robbery in progress came over the air. Korr and his partner sped to 163rd Street. A trembling robbery victim, directing them to a tenement house, said, "He just ran up the stairs." Korr raced into the building and moved toward the roof. As he reached the fourth floor landing two shots rang out. Korr retreated. Checking, he wasn't hit. Once again he moved upward. Seeing two flashes from above, Korr fired. The suspect fell wounded, hit in the leg. The rest was routine. Always a man to keep his own counsel, he neither showed nor expressed any lingering concern about the night's events when questioned.

Several weeks later, Korr was on routine patrol when his radio car came under rifle attack from a sniper. Korr leaped from the car, firing shots as he moved forward. Korr's courageous actions prevented the sniper from escaping. Trapped, the man surrendered. Case closed. Once again his reaction to the incident was stoical. "He's a cool customer," I remember Moe saying.

"Yea, but I'd like to know what's really going through his mind." Can a guy be that cool? I wondered.

It was several months later. Korr was walking alone on his foot post on 174th Street. Normally a busy street, the driving rain had emptied the block. Korr turned onto Vyse Avenue to have a smoke. While lighting the cigarette, he felt a prick in his leg and then heard the report of a rifle. He knew he was hit. As he slumped to the ground, he drew his revolver and fired in the direction of the shot. His mind was by now in complete chaos. Those previous incidents were all happening at once; he was bleeding to death. As fellow officers sped him to the hospital he kept saying, "I'm going to die, I'm going to die." The officers couldn't convince him otherwise. He had been in one gun battle too many. He was retired from the force on a medical disability.

Who will be next? Moe, me, Sergeant Saverin? Never, we say. It can only happen to others. But that's what Bill Korr thought, isn't it?

9

NIGHTS IN THE Four-one assumed bizarre characteristics. Take the night a probation officer got shot five times. An ambulance rushed him to Lincoln Hospital. When the report reached me, I decided to check on his situation. The usual Saturday night confusion reigned over the emergency room. Every time I went there I recalled that panoramic shot in *Gone with the Wind* which showed the Confederate wounded spread out over a railroad yard. At Lincoln, the scene is real.

A youth sprawled across a bench clutching a kitchen knife embedded six inches into his chest. His curses only inflated the babble of threats, anguished cries, adducements, moans of despair, and other expressions that are the everyday means of communication at that hospital. I passed a sobbing woman who clutched a bloodied towel. It covered one of her hands that no longer had four fingers. Three men groaned in a corner as they awaited treatment for gunshot wounds that had been diagnosed as nonfatal.

The probation officer lay in one of the ward's small operating rooms. As I watched through a small glass window, the nurses quickly stripped him. The doctors made a long incision down his chest and probed for the bullets. Skin was pulled aside like the pages of a newspaper. They dug, probed, cut, knotted, and sewed. For an hour the team labored over this man, anonymous to all of them. This was the best gunshot surgical team in the city. As in most professions, practice makes perfect. In this instance, however, their reward was death. Too much damage had been done by those .45 caliber bullets fired at close range. Now it was time to start filling out the required forms. At times it seems a man's destiny lies in a file cabinet.

Moe sat in the car clutching a transistor radio.

"How are the Yankees doing?" I asked as I slid in beside him.

"They lost 6-1."

"Shit. When is Stottlemyer going to get in the groove?"

"It's not his fault that he plays on the team with Bobby Murcer and seven other guys."

I nodded.

"A DOA, huh?"

"Yeah. He didn't have a chance."

"Do we call the family?"

"I spoke to probation. They want to do it. They'll call us at the station house."

"Any kids?"

"Five."

"Sonuvabitch." He hit the ignition and we moved toward 149th Street.

Cops have to laugh or they're lost. Some might think our humor perverse or macabre. Even in death we must find a means to release our horror, anger, fear, frustration. We can't cry so we laugh. Humor savagely makes sense out of otherwise intolerable situations.

As we turned onto 149th Street that night, a call came over the radio.

"Man out of the fourth floor window at 1460 Southern Boulevard – available Four-one unit," the dispatcher said calmly. So far, nothing new.

"Four-one, Henry. Central, we're on our way." That was Joe Hines in Sector Henry responding.

Seconds later, the radio crackled again. "Second man out window at 1460 Southern Boulevard."

Hines yelled, "We're on our way, Central." Moe and I perked up. This was getting interesting.

Central: "A third man just went out the same window."

We didn't speak. Moe gunned the car toward Southern Boulevard. Quiet for about 20 seconds. Then, "Fourth man out the fourth floor window."

An anonymous voice shouted over the radio, "Don't worry about it, Central, this whole fuckin' place is out the window." We laughed and our laughter rang solidly with the sound of truth.

At the scene, we found three men moaning in the alley behind the tenement. We made them as comfortable as possible while we waited for an ambulance. In the meantime, we found out what happened. A cousin, apparently a little unbalanced, tried to leave life by way of an open window. The three men tried to stop him. Instead, the three would-be rescuers found themselves being launched out the window, one by one, by the cousin. Then the cousin did his own number out the window. Only he didn't hurt himself. He got up and headed for Southern Boulevard.

As we placed the last man in the ambulance, someone shouted, "There he is." Sure enough, there he stood in the middle of the street, a T-shirted, dungareed, muscular man, insanely challenging buses, trucks, cars as they tried to avoid him. A toreador in Levi's. We ran toward him and at first he fled. Then he turned, imaginary lance in hand, and galloped at us. Moe hit high, I hit low. A classic two-on-one tackle.

133

When Moe finally cuffed him, he threw his hands up as if to stop the clock of some steer-roping contest. The crowd applauded; Moe bowed. The fantasy, whether his or ours, ended.

The duty captain pulled up alongside as the ambulance passed the red light on the corner. "Lieutenant, why don't you have your hat on," he yelled. I looked around the car, found it, and put it on. It sounded like something I might have worried about when I first arrived at the Four-one.

Moe laughed, but I was pissed off. "How do you like that bastard," I fumed. "Why don't they give those duty captains something to do. All they do is ride around pickin', pickin'. Did ya hear that silly bastard. They always mouth off before they know what the hell is going on." Moe laughed some more while I steamed.

We coasted back to the station house. Before we got there, a man stumbled out on the street waving his arms. I told Moe to pull over.

"What the hell we got now?" Moe said. "The guy looks stoned."

The man was a middle-aged Puerto Rican. "Hey, I been robbed," he yelled. "They take my money."

"Okay, calm down," I said. "What happened?"

"They take my money. Eighty-three dollars, my pay, all my money."

"Who took your money?"

"They did, in the cellar. They did." The man was near tears whether from anger or embarrassment, I couldn't tell.

We pulled the car over to the curb. "Okay," I said. "Show us." We followed the man across the street and into an alley.

The man pointed to a wooden staircase. "Down there, in the cellar," he said.

We told him to stay put and descended into the darkness. At the bottom we found a basement strewn with garbage. A locked wooden door led into the building. After pounding on it several times, we heard the latch being drawn. The face of a middle-aged woman appeared in the crack between the door and the door frame.

"A man says he was robbed here," I told her.

"I don't know nothing about any robbery," she said.

"All right if we look around?"

She hesitated and then nodded.

"Is this your apartment?" we asked.

"No, this belongs to Mr. Washington."

"Where's he?"

"In South Carolina, visiting his brother."

The place, quite literally, was a shit house. It was dark, dank, and it stunk like an overused latrine. Through it drifted the sweet smell of grass. A lot of things were going on in this place.

Derelicts dozed in the corners of the front room cradling their bottles in their arms. Further back, a hallway was lined with mattresses and on them sat two-dollar prostitutes waiting for the coins to drop. I pulled a curtain aside and saw a woman performing fellatio. The man grinned. "It's okay, brother. We're family," he said. The woman continued eagerly, indifferent to the audience. I turned away, sickened by the sordid atmosphere.

A short, barrel-chested man came rushing down the hall. He was obviously annoyed. "Look man, we're not looking for trouble, that man fulla shit. This be our home," he said.

"All right, all right," I said. "Come on outside. Let's straighten this out."

"Bullsheet. This is all bullsheet," the man said as we walked to the door. His attitude convinced me that there was something to the allegation. We went into the alley.

The drunk was still there. "Recognize these people?" I asked him.

"I don't see anyone. It dark. I go in with a woman. Someone rob me."

"Wait a minute. You picked up a pross on the corner and she brought you here?" The stocky man shut up. He stared at the drunk with apprehension.

"Please, Officer. I want my money. I want my eighty-three dollar."

"Do you want these people arrested? Can you point out who robbed you?"

"No. No. I want my money."

"Okay," I said. "Here's what I'm gonna do. I'm gonna walk out of the alley. Either you guys straighten this out or I'm gonna turn it over to the detectives." Some tough guy, I thought as Moe and I walked away from the drunk and the stocky man.

We could hear the voices but not what was said.

"Don't ever come back here, ya bastard," the stocky man finally yelled.

"Now, boys," I yelled. "Let's be gentle." Moe and I grinned. This little comedy had reached its happy ending.

As the drunk came over to us he held out a ten-dollar bill.

"You don't learn fast, do you?" Moe said.

"Look, mister," I said. "You have any kids."

He nodded. "Three."

"You have a nice wife."

He nodded again.

I hated playing righteous priest to his repentant sinner, but the guy had been lucky. Next time he might wash a similar alley with his blood.

"Then do all of us a favor and don't mess around with pigs like that anymore. Take the ten and buy your kids a toy or something." The man mumbled thanks and walked away, straining for some sense of equilibrium.

Moe and I made a note to tell the Division Public Morals Squad about this place. Not that it would do any good. In a neighborhood like this, all they needed was a dark cellar and some mattresses. And some dumb Johns who thought a night of fun could be bought for a few bucks.

Cops aren't very fond of prostitutes; they create work. Either the community is complaining of their presence, or some John is claiming to have been ripped off, or a prostitute is claiming she was raped. We harass, chase, and arrest them, but the courts let them out the same night. It's nearly impossible to get rid of them. The best you can do is to force them to find another location, hopefully in another precinct. The only value a prostitute has for policemen is that she's an excellent source of information. The prostitutes in the Four-one bear no resemblance to Shirley McLaine's Irma La Douce. They are the ugliest assortment of hes, shes, he-shes, and she-hes in the world. They do very well.

Not more than ten minutes later, another man waved us down. He pointed toward a nearby street corner. "That whore, she stole my wallet," he yelled.

We got out of the car, but as soon as the woman saw us, she dropped the wallet. Apparently she didn't have time to pilfer the contents; the man's identification and money were recovered.

"Damn prostitutes. They no fuckin' good," he said as he counted his money.

I wasn't through playing priest. "You didn't think that half an hour ago," I said. I'm glad I chose to be a cop. I would have made a lousy priest. The message didn't sink in.

To my surprise, the station house was quiet when we returned. No riots, no demonstrations, no angry words protesting an arrest. It's not normal, I said to myself. It wasn't.

A girl sat in a corner quietly crying. She was young and she was white, which was unusual. I had heard the sound of tears many times before, tears of loss, anguish, frustration, tears that come when a mighty fear is lifted, tears of gratitude. Hers came after a great effort had been made to choke them back. Now she shed them in the barren muster room of the Four-one, and she was very alone.

"What's with her?" I asked the desk sergeant.

He tried to be as matter-of-fact as possible. "She's a VISTA volunteer. She's been here two months, working with some local people. Tonight was the second time she's been raped."

"The second time?" Are there any limits, I asked myself. I didn't even bother to wait for an answer.

"Yeah. She thought it was one of those things the first time, one of the hazards of being here. She thought that eventually she could gain some sort of acceptance." He shook his head. "Now she wants to go home."

"Where's home?"

"Nebraska. Council Bluffs, Nebraska, to be exact."

I have never been to Nebraska. For that matter, I doubt that many people from Nebraska have visited the South Bronx. While I'm sure there are rapes in Nebraska, and murders and other forms of violence that are such a popular part of American life, I couldn't help but share the sergeant's sense of disdain. To come all this way, like some righteous missionary, without any apparent regard for the consequences of life in the ghetto was not only reckless but a trifle stupid. A long time ago, I felt sorry for most social workers. Now I wished they would just go away, or at least confine their activities to the old and the ill. What people need are jobs. Until serious changes are made in many areas of our social and economic life, we will pay the price in crime.

Sure, I felt outrage. But tragedy, genuine tragedy, needs some guise of nobility and there was no nobility in the Four-one. So while Moe fetched the girl a Coke and I offered commiseration, I hoped that she would return safely to Nebraska. I respected her idealism but knew how misspent it was. Hopefully, her experience here would not leave a permanent scar.

She didn't know the rapist and gave a sketchy description. It was put over the air but the search was fruitless. The case was turned over to the detectives.

Back at the desk I asked the sergeant if probation had called.

"Funny thing about that, Lou," he said. "We did a background check on the guy. Five arrests including one for robbery and assault."

"We're talking about the same guy?" I asked. "The probation officer who was shot and died tonight at Lincoln?"

"The same guy."

"You mean the ex-cons are leading the ex-cons?"

He nodded. "That's what Downtown gives us. This job isn't far behind. We're starting to get rookies with records."

"But not with robbery and assault convictions. Could be he's a phony. Maybe he glommed the badge and the I.D."

"No, he's their man."

"Well, it doesn't matter now-he's dead."

I turned away from the desk. Most of the time I felt only helpless; now I felt confused. How long before felons wore badges? How soon before prosecution became impossible because too many clogged our jails? Simple questions asked many times before, I knew. I yelled to Moe, "Hey, how about stopping after work." Maybe a couple of brews would lift me up.

Moe grinned at me. "Great idea, Lou," he said. "We can talk about duty captains."

So at two in the morning we sat in a bar called Happy's, a relatively safe place because it was frequented by off-duty policemen. The beers were cool, the conversation light and irreverent. And just a short distance away, a young man named Raymond Santago, ambled slowly down Westchester Avenue.

Five members of a gang that had christened itself "the Warlocks" figured him an easy mark for a mugging. They stalked him. He staggered, he stumbled. A drunk is easiest to take. Most times he doesn't remember a thing. They encircled him and moved closer.

No wonder they stood stunned when he turned and faced them, a knife in one hand, a gun in the other. He struck swiftly at the youth nearest him, plunging the knife into his chest, killing him instantly. Mesmerized, the gang watched as Santiago ran and hopped down the street.

By the time they recovered, it was too late for direct action. They followed him as best they could, warily, uneasily. This was not the night they had hoped for.

Santiago led them to the shack of a gypsy cab company directly across from Happy's. Finally the drivers called the Four-one for help. Our units arrived and surrounded the place. Hearing the sirens, Santiago fled to the rear of the building and barricaded himself, as best he could, in a small bathroom.

Moe and I, of course, heard the commotion and trotted to the street. A crowd had quickly gathered. We crossed the lines and joined Lieutenant Bill Stillman and his sergeant, Art Johnson, who were in charge. As we got there, Stillman was saying, "Let's try to talk him out. Maybe we'll get lucky."

They went into the office and tried to persuade Santiago to surrender. His responses were in Spanish. Stillman asked one of the gypsy drivers to convey his pleas. No luck. Apparently convinced that he had no other recourse, Santiago remained. If he was trying to prove his manhood, it was the wrong time and the wrong place.

Emergency Service was called. They responded with special equipment: shotguns and bulletproof vests. In this instance they probably wouldn't be needed. But precautions were always necessary.

After examining the situation, Johnson argued against their use. "The hall's too narrow," he said. "Men with vests and shotguns will never be able to maneuver there." Stillman and Johnson looked at one another, knowing that Johnson was right. "I'll go after him," Johnson finally said.

The lieutenant said he wanted time to think it over. The sergeant proposed a dangerous course. Stillman had every confidence in Johnson, but a move undetected, a shot fired quickly and true could leave him with a dead officer to explain. I knew the feeling. I've been there before.

Stillman said to Johnson, "Okay. Go in." Holy shit. John Wayne couldn't have done it better.

Two officers covered Johnson as he crept down the hall. Each crouched at opposite ends of the hall. They watched the door patiently, waiting for some sign of movement. None came.

Johnson practically crawled the last fifteen yards. Bracing one hand on the floor and the other on the wall, he dragged his legs forward so that his pistol always remained pointed at the door. Once he reached the door, he assumed a squatting position. Anyone bursting out would have missed him at first, giving him a chance to get off a shot.

Half the hallway was in shadow. It smelt faintly of urine, like a subway underpass. This singular effect, I suppose, kept all concerned firmly rooted in reality. We knew we were still in the Bronx and not in some West Coast sound studio.

To adequately cover Johnson, a couple of men edged their way down the hall. It was a gutsy but necessary act. Johnson reached up, turned the knob, and pushed on the door. It gave about a half an inch.

He rested a moment. Johnson's backup men moved closer. Then Johnson leaned back and gave the door a shove. No one was visible. Johnson hesitated.

Then Santago jumped at him from behind the partially closed shower curtain. Collapsing against a wall, Johnson heard the knife swish by his head. His pistol barked three times; Santago, like a running back caught by a knee-high tackle, fell forward with three slugs in his legs. He was removed to Lincoln Hospital.

Moe and I went back to our beers. Better than a double feature at the RKO on Fordham Road. Seriously, we weighed Johnson's chances and figured they were about the same as a wounded lion's against a pack of hungry hyenas. Too often I had seen and heard of incidents where the officer breaks the door down à la Jack Webb and then his face disappears courtesy of a .375 magnum or a shotgun. It isn't pretty, but it's real. Johnson took a hell of a chance. Not often is bravery rewarded with life's greatest prize – your own skin.

Time for the flip side. A few nights later, the dispatcher comes on. "I have a lady at 985 Kelly who says that two white males are carrying her refrigerator down the stairs." We laughed. "They're between the third and second floor landings," the dispatcher says.

"Sector Ida will go," says a voice.

"Is there any beer in it?" another voice asked.

Minutes later, Sector Ida was back on the radio. The voice was strong but patient. "Central," it said. "Have a bus respond to 985 Kelly. I have two drunks trapped under a refrigerator on the second floor landing." Life started to look up.

Four-thirty in the morning and all was quiet. Moe talked about conservation and rats. A hunter, Moe is well versed in conservation. Tonight his subject was rats. Since they were the most prevalent domesticated animal in the Four-one, whether the owners knew it or not, it was interesting to hear him defend them. It seems they eat a lot of garbage which is the precinct's principal export. Moe made them sound like sanitary engineers. In keeping with the mayor's program of painting everything in the sanitation department white, I could see the rats scurrying about in white smocks. Then there was the possibility of giving them six-toed surgical gloves. We could arrange for a delivery service, turn the Four-one into a huge Third Avenue deli. Wrap the garbage in individual green paper bags and throw in free dill pickles. Our minds clacked like an uptown express.

I'm not sure I heard the shot. I saw the flash. Bluish white, from a window to our left. We were on Fox Street and it is narrow and we had no room to maneuver. "Get the hell out of here," I screamed at Moe as I dropped down in the front seat. "He'll take the numbers right off your badge."

A second shot ricocheted off the sidewalk as Moe buried his foot into the floor. I gabbed the radio and told Central to send two cars, one for each end of the block. But we knew it would be too late.

Moe stopped about 100 yards down the street. We backtracked, sticking to the shadows. We moved to a building three doors from the one we wanted and hit the roof. We moved cautiously over the roofs. Reaching the building we wanted, we moved slowly downward. The apartment where the shots had come from was vacant. "Creepy," one of the patrolmen said. "I had it happen to me twice. If you don't get hit, you forget it in a couple of days. " I knew I wouldn't. Moe and I tried to stay off Fox Street unless there was a call, but like an unfriendly neighbor it was impossible to avoid. I felt very low that night.

10

WE CAN'T AFFORD to let our lives be consumed by depression. Like most people, cops seek diversion, ways to relax. Some, with large families and expenses to meet, cannot afford the luxury of complete relaxation. They moonlight; push cabs, become successful electricians or house painters or, as in Moe's case, ironworkers. Some of us try retreating with the family. We find summer homes for quiet weekends, we pursue hobbies, we do anything to get away from the Four-one. And then, of course, there's Happy's.

Stand in Grand Central or Penn Station sometime around rush hour and watch the weary commuters crowd the bar. It's no different for cops. Only we have to be more selective. I've never heard this thought expressed explicitly in the Department, but a man I know who was once a military policeman said that in one of his training lectures, he was instructed to go only to those bars frequented by other MP's. It makes sense. You don't want to run into a guy you busted twelve hours earlier. And, while relaxing with your beer, you don't want to have one eye open for possible malfeasances. So you go to a bar where other cops go, a bar that likes cops and won't tread too heavily on the sensibilities of the law. Such a place is Happy's.

One laughable thing struck me as I read past reports concerning incidents in Happy's. Take this mythical example.

At approximately 0335 hours on June 7, 1972 Patrolman Lance Havenot, Shield 39466, 41st Precinct, arrested one Rex Prince of 741 Fox Street for the robbery of Happy's Bar, 2611 Westchester Avenue.

Patrolman Havenot performed a 1600 to 2400 hours tour on June 6, 1972 and then proceeded to his residence at 0025 hours. Upon arrival at his residence at 0100 hours, he realized that he had left his house keys in his locker and returned to the precinct to retrieve them. He arrived at the station house at 0135 hours. He decided, once back at the station house, to make out his monthly activity report which was due on June 10, 1972. At 0250 hours he was once again proceeding north along Westchester Avenue toward his residence when he got a flat tire. He fixed the flat and continued north again. The time was 0335 hours. Upon passing Happy's Bar he noticed a white male, later identified as Rex Prince, standing behind the bar, who was unfamiliar to him. He decided to investigate. (Report goes on to tell about the capture.)

What does paragraph two above really mean? Please pick A, B, C, or D.

A. Patrolman Havenot had a lot of problems after finishing his tour of duty.

B. Patrolman Havenot is an alert patrolman.

C. Patrolman Havenot should carry an extra set of keys, get rid of his bald tires, and prepare his reports on time.

D. Patrolman Havenot stopped at Happy's for a couple of beers.

The fourth answer is the correct one. But the investigator would never just come out and say, "Patrolman Havenot felt like a couple of beers after work and stopped at Happy's." It was just *verboten*. The writer would spend half a page to get around that fact. It's the Let's-protect-ourselves-syndrome. After a while you need a Bureaucratic Report Analyst to interpret what the writer means. The unfortunate part about this type of lapse is that once the truth is prostituted for appearance' sake the credibility of the entire report is undermined. I think it's something we have been conditioned to do over the years. It was due to the highly moralistic and righteous attitude emanating from Headquarters. It is a carryover from the John Walsh, Irish Mafia control of the department. Thus, field officers hesitated to put into their reports very innocent, innocuous, and common happenings lest an uptight Headquarters construe it as a sign of decadence in the colonies and start one of their ritual witch-hunts against the parties involved. Social gambling and dating are the two other most common categories where field commanders are found to be less than candid with Headquarters. It must be said, however, that the present administration is moving in the right direction.

To reach Happy's from the Four-one, you had to pass several junkie and prostitute bars. It's a quiet place on Westchester Avenue. Besides cops, bus drivers, and cabbies, Happy's clientele reflected the ethnic mix of the area: the remaining whites, mainly Irish and Jews; Puerto Ricans; and blacks. Happy's projected a pleasant ambiance and you could always count on meeting a friend or two. For a lot of men, single and married, life in the Four-one included an orbit around Happy's, although some men came to regret that affiliation.

Take Patrolmen Cola and Kaster. They had been partners for a couple of years. Drinkers and brawlers both, they always handled their jobs well. In some instances too well, such as using their fists in confrontations with area gangs. Rather than make arrests and press charges they preferred to beat heads.

One day, during their lunch hour, they parked their car behind Happy's, went in, and had their "one-foot-on-the-rail" lunch. They usually liked an early meal but this day they were scheduled late. Much to their delight, the radio picked up just as they "10-63'd" (permission to take the break). Standing in the air-conditioned bar, they sipped their beers and joked with a few old-timers.

After quite awhile, radio cars screamed by outside, sirens whining. A fire truck barreled by and then more patrol cars. Kaster remarked to his partner that "it sounds like the end of the world out there." He wanted to take a look but Cola cautioned him, "If the world ends while I'm on my meal break, I don't give a shit." They hunched further over the bar and soaked up two more cold ones.

The disturbance outside had reached such a peak that Kaster finally decided to take a look. He got as far as the door. As he opened it, the heat and noise pushed him back. "What the hell," he said. "Give me another beer."

Several minutes later, Sergeant Saverin appeared at the door. He waved to the two men. Cola waved back and yelled, "Come on in, Sarge, and have one." Saverin's movements became more animated but he remained by the door.

"The idiot," Cola said. "He doesn't even understand sign language."

"An Italian who doesn't understand sign language. That is strange," Kaster remarked.

They sipped their beers for a minute. "I guess we ought to see what he wants," Cola said finally.

They put on their hats and worked their way to the door, straightening ties, tucking their shirts in. As they opened the door they met the reason for Saverin's refusal to recognize their hand signals. Behind him stood the captain, his face so red you could have sold him for $1.59 a pound.

"You guys have had it this time," Saverin whispered. "You were due back from meal 35 minutes ago. That's when the shit hit the fan."

Cola retained his wits. "Look, Sarge, we only took our hour. Then Happy called us about fifteen minutes ago to make a complaint about some junkies that were hanging around. We were just in there checking things out."

Saverin paused as though considering the explanation.

"What's the problem? Why don't we just get back on patrol and get the job done?"

The sergeant smiled and nodded.

Cola and Kaster walked briskly, professionally past the captain, pleased with their escape. As they rounded the corner, Kaster was saying, "You're fantastic, just fantastic. That's the second time this set that you've talked us out of trouble." Both men stopped in their tracks.

"Where's the car?" Cola asked. Then they spotted it, or what was left of it. The vehicle was now a twisted, blackened hunk of metal, burned almost beyond recognition and certainly beyond use. It still cast a pall of smoke across the lot.

The captain and the sergeant walked around the corner. "We got a report a gang of kids set it up about 25 minutes ago; 10 minutes after you came back from meal, right?" the captain said.

This time Cola was silent, and Kaster looked at him as if expecting some glib, face-saving answer. None came. Saverin finally said, "Sometimes nothing helps, not even Italian hand signals." The captain shook his head. Charges were preferred against the two officers and they each lost five days' pay.

The presence of policemen did not make Happy's a sanctuary. One man, while on duty, tried to arrest two disorderly men only to be attacked in turn with hunting knives. They forced him to shoot his way out.

But by far the closest call in Happy's happened to a patrolman named Jerry Creek. Creek, a young black officer, stopped off one night to see the boys. Eight of us had been there earlier, but we left for my house to play some poker. (I had been living in Co-op City about four months and my wife and family were visiting my mother-in-law at her summer place for a couple of days.) We invited Creek to the game but gave up on him when he hadn't reached Happy's by 1 A.M.

As Creek entered the bar, he noticed several things were out of place. For one thing, there was no sound; the jukebox sat mute, no conversation flowed across the bar. And the customers were all still, staring straight ahead, their hands flat on the bar. Then again, there was the man who quickly shoved a shotgun toward his face. Creek froze. Two other men waving revolvers stood behind him.

As directed, he took his place along the bar. A quick search followed and the men found his .38 caliber Smith and Wesson. The man with the shotgun grinned but not without nervousness. "Hey, man, I think we've got a motherfuckin' pig here, a real live motherfuckin' pig." Creek said nothing. "Let's blow the motherfucker away," the man said.

Creek nearly offered some blithe remark about his pure regard for his mother when he heard the hammer of the shotgun being cocked. "Hey, man," he said, scared as hell and trying to sound it. "I'm no pig mother. I'm a guard. I'm too short to be a pig." He felt the cold blue metal against his neck. "Honest, brothers I'm just a guard."

One of the robbers turned to the bartender. "Do you know this cat?"

Happy nodded. "Yeah, he's a guard." The robbers nodded and the shotgun was withdrawn. They told Creek to have a drink and act naturally. Creek hoped they would consider shaking a natural form of behavior for him.

Then the three went down the bar, collecting a little over $500 from the patrons and the bar cash register. By this time Creek's relief at the success of his ploy turned to anger. He felt degraded by the extorted lie. On top of that, they had his gun.

In the movies, they make a big thing about someone taking a cop's badge from him. For most of us, it's that weapon we don't like to lose. At that moment, Creek became determined to bust the three crooks.

When they fled the bar, Creek was close behind. Running to the corner of Hoe Avenue, they stopped a gypsy cab and commandeered it. Jumping into his own car, Creek gave chase. On his way up Hoe, he spotted Sector Henry. In the car were Patrolmen Tom Roark and Bill White. Roark, the driver, was one of the real "jocks" of the precinct. He enjoyed nothing more than a wild chase through narrow streets. The precinct leader when it came to accidents, he was eventually grounded for the protection of citizens and fellow officers alike. When they heard Creek's story and description of the vehicle and men, they shot off, followed by the determined Creek.

The gypsy cab headed west toward the Four-two. White grabbed the radio as much for support as communication. Roark was into his number now – lights on, weaving erratically, maneuvering to miss double-parked cars, push-carts, ice cream trucks, telephone poles, phone booths, and fire hydrants. Yes, fire hydrants.

Creek had never witnessed such a frightening display of inept driving. Robbers in gypsy cabs sometimes outmaneuvered police cars, but how in the hell do you get away from a nut like Roark? The three thieves must have reached the same conclusion; they abandoned the cab and hit the alleys.

As they ran in front of the policemen, White opened fire. Then he and Roark decided to pursue the one with the shotgun. The man hustled into an abandoned building. As they closed in, he opened fire. The sound of any gun can be a frightening thing, but nothing is quite so nerve-shattering as a shotgun bursting down a darkened street. Still unarmed, Creek timed his move for the period between shots when the gunman had to reload. He charged into the building, raced recklessly down the hall, and caught the man at the staircase trying to jam two shells into the breech of his gun. Almost instinctively, Creek said later, he dove for the man's knees and brought him down. A knee and then a foot to the face followed. Swollen with anger, Creek continued to pummel the man long after the fight left him. Roark and White gently but insistently pulled him off. The search continued for the other two but with no results. His composure recovered, along with his gun, Creek went back to Happy's and bought the proprietor a couple of beers.

Not all the incidents revolving around Happy's reach happy resolutions. Take the case of Patrolman Ramon Wista. One day he returned from an appearance in court and decided to try option number two. Option number one was to work the rest of his shift, but that prospect didn't appeal to him. Option number two was to request a foot post on Southern Boulevard, hit Happy's for a couple of Gibsons, deposit his personal effects in Happy's safe, and then head for the apartment of a girl named Rosita. There had been rumors in the Four-one that Downtown had declared Happy's off-limits, so he bought a pint and carried it to the girl's flat.

Rosita and Ramon enjoyed a long friendship; many a pleasant hour was spent in her apartment. She was a rather unprepossessing woman whose main assets were youth (twenty-five years old), marital status (single), and availability (very available). Since he had married a very attractive girl six months earlier, most of his fellow officers couldn't understand his infatuation with Rosita. His fellow officers' disapprobation notwithstanding, Wista kept his assignation with Rosita, then drifted off to sleep.

While he slept, Rosita noticed that his wallet had fallen out of his pocket. For most people, wallets, like other people's mail, fascinate. She explored the wallet and came up with a picture of Mrs. Wista along with a handwritten note of affection.

Wista slept peacefully as Rosita contemplated his betrayal of her. Finally she called Mrs. Wista and told her where to collect her rotten husband. Then Mrs.

Wista called the station house and spoke with the sergeant. He told her to come to the precinct and they would visit the love nest together.

In the meantime, the sergeant called me off patrol. Rosita welcomed us at the door and led us to the room where the nude patrolman Wista slept, his face still reflecting contentment. Until we awoke him, he had never considered the possibility of losing three things: his wife, his job and his mistress. I reserve judgment except to say that he made some dumb moves. Perhaps he wanted to get caught all along. All I know is that when I shook his shoulder he shot out of bed as if I had shoved a hot spoon between his buttocks. His attempt to stand at attention was most unconvincing. We politely escorted him back to the station house. After an administrative hearing, he was dropped from the Department.

A regular at Happy's was a guy named Bill Stevens. He had lived for many years in the area and owned his own garage at the northern end of the precinct. Many a night Bill helped close Happy's with some men from the precinct. Affable, with a sharp wit and a penchant for strong cigars and good stories, he made many evenings more pleasurable by his presence.

This particular night, after closing the bar, several officers accompanied him back to his garage. He faced a long day and he wanted to get an early start on a special customer's car.

That customer, a man named Harvey Green, arrived in the early afternoon. Bill had been under the vehicle all morning trying to correct a problem with the transmission. Angry that the job remained undone, Green demanded his car. The two men quarreled for several minutes with Bill saying he needed another day to finish the job properly. Finally he gave in and returned from his office with the car keys and a bill for the work already done. The car wouldn't start. This infuriated Green who drew a pistol and fired at Bill, hitting him several times.

His overalls streaked with blood, Bill staggered out onto the sidewalk and collapsed. Following him, Green stood over the prone victim, aimed the pistol once more, and pulled the trigger. Nothing. An empty gun. Green then removed a set of keys from Bill's pocket. He ran back to the garage, jumped into Bill's Cadillac, and drove down the ramp and into the street.

A crowd gathered; several men ran to nearby phones. Trying to get to his feet Bill staggered further into the street. At that moment the Cadillac, in full flight, stopped. Tires squealed as Green threw the big car into reverse. Frozen, the crowd watched as he backed the car at full speed, gears whining, down the block. They heard the deep clunk, a sound like a trunk lid closing, as the rear tires passed over the body. Green shifted into drive, revved the engine, and completed the job. With tires still squealing, he sped away.

Patrolmen Coan and Fry responded. Searching Bill's body, they came up with a registration form. Matching the information on it with the description of onlookers, they came up with a plate number and quickly broadcast it.

Moe had taken the day off to go fishing and John Arm took over as my driver. We were cruising down

Garrison Avenue when we heard the call. "We're on his tail going south on Bruckner Boulevard toward the Four-o," we heard Sergeant Von Kling yell. Since Garrison runs parallel to Bruckner, I told John to step on it. We were in a position to intercept. Unfortunately the car wasn't. It lost power. We hit Bruckner just as the Cadillac sped past with Von Kling in pursuit. Several other cars helped to cut Green off, however, and Von Kling easily subdued the man. The car ran smoothly for the rest of the tour. Enough said.

I told Moe about it the next day and he laughed. "So you missed your Italian wheelman?" he said. Needless to say, many of us were angered by Bill's murder. His kind don't come around more than once.

For those of us with families or pressing financial needs, the ups and downs of Happy's were a very sometime thing. Instead we turned to moonlighting. I have known officers who moonlight as psychiatrists, chiropractors, chiropodists, pharmacists, physicists, lawyers, professors, teachers, businessmen, bakers, laborers, and cabbies. In many instances this choice of a second profession, even of a career, shows a degree of creativity cops are seldom given credit for. And tenacity. For a man to work a full shift and then plunk his butt down in the front seat of a cab for nine more hours takes a lot of staying power.

I have personally worked as a teacher, chemist, cabbie, postal worker, laborer, and plumber since joining the force. In the Four-one we had, among others: floorwaxers, a group that formed their own painting company, a part-time janitor at a school near his home, a baby photographer, a man who owns his own air-conditioning business, a few mechanics, several bartenders, a children's clothing salesman, a longshoreman, a soda salesman, a hotel manager, several stock-market traders (although they might be back in the cab business now), and a guy who sells Sesame Street games. He claims that if you use his records, you will definitely pass the sergeant's exam. And so on.

For example, there is O. J. O. J. was the unofficial leader of those men who moonlight as cabbies. He and his men were especially proud of the fact that policemen moonlighting as cabbies had apparently helped cut the taxi crime rate. In 1970, eight cabbies were slain. The following year, when officers were encouraged to work as cabbies, none were killed. Many felt that the unknown factor of an off-duty cop in the front seat of the hack was responsible.

O. J. is a cheerful, buoyant Irishman who some call "the Leprechaun." When I heard of him, he had been pushing a hack for over four years. He liked driving nights, the most convenient time for his schedule and the best time to hustle.

In the cab business, hustling is half the work. There's nothing romantic about the job. Spend eight or nine or even twelve hours in the front seat of one of those yellow monsters for more than a year and I'll guarantee you curvature of the spine. Once on the street it's cutthroat and a job lost is money out of your pocket. Want to know what I mean? Someday stand at the corner of, say 52nd and Third at 11 A.M. and watch the cabs. At that time of day, the office workers are in their offices and the shoppers are shopping. Lift your hand to brush back your hair or wave to a friend and you could cause a nine-way traffic accident in living yellow.

The same thing is true at 10 P.M. Dinner is over, the theaters are packed, the streets are empty, your pocket is empty, you're beginning to feel desperate. But don't get me wrong, the enemy isn't the public; it's that damn clock.

On the dashboard of all New York cabs sits a meter. Cabbies call it a clock. As instruments go, it is reasonably accurate. But since it, like the cab in many cases, is the property of the owner it is also the cabbies' number one enemy. Figure it this way. At the time I drove, the owner got 51 percent of what the clock registered. If, as the owners claimed during the most recent strike, cabbies make around $150 a week including tips, that means a cabby has to pull in around $51 per day on the clock – $26 for the owner, $25 for himself. That's not including at least $5 a day in tips. To make that much money, $30 a day, the driver has to book over twenty-five trips. But is that the cabby's average day? Given luck, the weather, the state of your stomach, and the condition of your hack, the answer is no. A total take of $30 a day is more realistic. So you fight the clock. It's the only way to survive.

In the old days, it was simple. You'd make a deal with a rider. Pick up a fare at Sheridan Square who wants to go to 42nd Street and you tell the passenger it will cost $1.50. If he or she agrees, you leave the "flag" up. For the owner's purposes, the cab is still unoccupied. You pocket the $1.50 and in many instances the rider got a bargain. Cabbies call this "highflagging," or "riding on the arm."

It didn't take long for the owners to discover the practice. At first they tracked down the more flagrant "highflaggers" simply by comparing total mileage with mileage recorded while the meter was on. But this didn't catch the nickel-and-dimers, the guys out for only five or six extra dollars a shift, the O.J.'s of this world. So the owners brought in the "hot seat."

This is, essentially, a device connecting the five passenger seats of the cab with the meter. If you weigh 20 pounds or more and sit on that seat for approximately 15 seconds, the meter flicks on. The driver has no control over it. This development meant a virtual end to highflagging, to taking the wife shopping, to giving friends brief rides. Also, it made mistakes all the more painful such as when a downtown trip hops in about the time you want to go home, which is uptown. First there's the argument over who is going where, and then when the guy steps back out, the meter flips over, and you're out 65¢, the city tax. It also cuts into the out-of-town jobs that can be quite lucrative if you have the time. A guy wants to go to Greenwich, Connecticut, and you strike a bargain and all the way there he watches the meter and fumes. Without the hot seat, at least the poor guy didn't have to watch himself get taken. Of course, none of them understood that you have to allow for the empty trip home.

All of this entered O.J.'s mind when he first encountered the "hot seat." He saw his earnings drop $20 for a ten-hour shift. At a special meeting, O.J. urged revolution and the removal of the device. Unfortunately he was voted down, 23-2. The man who agreed with him, one Billy Butterworth, joined O.J. on a crusade against the "hot seat."

First they built a wooden platform which they fit over the back seat of the cab. In theory, it negated the "hot seat" since riders didn't really sit on the seat at all. In practice, many riders refused to sit on the uncomfortably hard surface just so O. J. could make a few extra bucks.

So he added cushions. This was fine except the rider had to be under five feet, five inches tall or else his head would be constantly pummeled by the roof. O. J. faced a simple choice: find a better method or cruise the streets looking for midgets or at least very short people.

He came up with a suspended cushion seat that seemed to work well on the passenger side of the front seat. This seat, however, negated whatever security was offered by the Plexiglas partition between the front and back seats. But O. J. felt he had his answer. He spent much of his time cajoling people to sit up front, so much so that he finally dubbed the invention his "come-on-up" seat.

To protect himself, he avoided ghetto areas and resisted passengers he thought might take him to ghetto areas – which eliminated most of the non-white minority groups in the city. Imagine his surprise when he invited a friendly, round-faced little white man into the front seat of his cab and was promptly bopped by a blackjack. While lying unconscious, $40 was taken.

When he got out of the hospital, he was more determined than ever to beat the system. He wrote a letter to the manufacturer asking for certain specifications. Then, with the help of an electrician, he worked his way around the problem. To this day, he refuses to divulge his solution. "You slobs accepted the hot seat, now you live with it," he said. In his own obsessive way, O. J. asserted his individuality.

Moe, as I have said, is an ironworker. One night, when things were relatively quiet and we were enjoying a break, I asked him about a typical day.

"Usually I hit the local union hall early in the morning," he said. "Like the other morning, I saw Tom, he's a representative, and he said there were four jobs available; a stair job, a window erection, a railing job, and a platform job. I asked him if he had any jobs in Manhattan because I like the atmosphere in the city. And the girl-watching isn't bad either.

"But he told me the platform job would be better. It was a foreman's job which meant it would be easier than most and it was at Schaefer Beer in Brooklyn which probably meant all the beer we could drink.

"Being foreman meant I could pick my own men. So I called 'the Bird,' he's an old friend, at home and told him to hustle down to Schaefer. I mentioned that it was a two-day job and he should look the part. Tom gave me two more guys and the three of us headed for Brooklyn.

"When I saw 'the Bird' with his roach-kicking shoes and pressed pants, I was mad. He didn't even look like an ironworker.

"The general super was waiting for us. He gave 'the Bird' some very funny looks while we went over the blueprints. But everything seemed all right. The way things are today, even hard-hats have long hair and a lot of them you can't tell from the hippies.

"Anyway, we were supposed to take out an old plat-form. That meant the first day we were mostly burning. They kept a refrigerator nearby loaded with beer, and it was hot, and needless to say we opened and closed the door a lot. At lunchtime they rolled a keg out for us. It was a good day – we all got bombed.

" 'The Bird's' wife was angry when she saw him in such a polluted state. Then she saw his paycheck. Since then, he's been encouraged to work with me."

We might have laughed louder but behind all the stories lay some dismal truths. To raise a family, especially in the city, and live in a relatively safe neighborhood, the average cop has to generate extra income. And if this meant pushing a hack or doing ironworking, then they would do it.

Then there was Harry Gold who loved animals. He worked in a pet shop in Brooklyn, made some connections, and then went into wholesaling. He imported rare species of birds and crocodiles from Africa until the Government caught him. Chagrined, the Department put its own pressure on him; at which point, Harry resigned. Currently, he is an affluent businessman in Brooklyn. One of my fellow officers, Phil Gonzalez, recently purchased a boa constrictor from him. Phil keeps the snake in a cage in his apartment. He hunts and traps rats in buildings around the precinct. The snake eats the catch and, given the state of the precinct, I have no doubt that Phil reaps a bountiful harvest for his pet. He claims this scene turns his girl friends on. If you ever met his girl friends, you would understand.

––––––––––

Most officers do not consider the next moonlighter very interesting or colorful. This is probably because only a few people know anything about him. He is "the Oracle," an apprentice undertaker. He picked up the nickname because of his sideline and his penchant for incorrectly predicting future moves by the Department. He says that in another two years he will be able to open his own funeral parlor. A very pleasant, quiet, and retiring individual, he is also one hell of a lousy cop. The Oracle's abilities always bring to mind how Sherlock Holmes had wanted to write a monograph on malingering. The Oracle could have easily co-authored the work with Holmes. He's always walking around in a trance, which brings up a more interesting facet of the man. One day, I was discussing Sir Arthur Conan Doyle's flirtation with the spiritual world with a couple of guys. I have read everything in the library written by or about Sir Arthur. The Oracle overheard the conversation and before long the two of us were engaged in a fascinating conversation about the occult. It was during this discussion that he told me about his own flirtation. Every Wednesday night, if he is off, he goes to Brooklyn to attend a seance. He claims his group (all city employees) has communicated with some of the most famous people in the Other World.

The Oracle had planted a seed in my mind which was to blossom into one of my most unforgettable experiences at the Fort. One day he asked me if I would like to attend one of his group's seances. I accepted. He said that he would have to get the permission of his group first, which he finally received after a two-week wait. He said that it would be necessary, since I was an outsider, for me to be blindfolded before reaching the location. I agreed.

I met him at the station house the following Wednesday at 8 P.M. I had decided to play detective long before my arrival at the station house. I smelled a challenge and the Oracle seemed to be offering one. As we drove toward our destination I noted that the Oracle never went over 55 m.p.h. on the highway, and that while driving through the sidestreets he averaged around 30 m.p.h. When we arrived in Brooklyn, he stopped the car and put a hood over my head. I made a mental note of the location. I had counted to 2,342 before the car stopped and I was helped out. I had also recognized several familiar sounds as we drove, and I cataloged them. The cool, moist air and the crumpling of leaves as I walked reminded me of New England. The cool air surprised me as it had been a rather warm drive. I heard an iron gate opening in front of me and then closing behind me. The place was damp, cold, and musty. I was placed in a chair and the hood was removed. It was pitch black except for the small candle which was sitting on top of a slab of concrete, made into a table by two wooden horses. As my eyes adjusted to the dark, I noticed the outlines of seven other people also sitting around the concrete table. It was impossible to see anything else. The figure at my right rose and ordered everyone to join hands and pray. The prayers they offered were like no others I had ever heard. They were weird and had little meaning for me. I was telling myself what a stupid bastard I was to be here. The leader, who was to be the medium, then asked us to meditate as he was going to try to raise a spirit. After about five minutes, the leader began to moan softly. It was weird, if nothing else. The leader started to talk, but this time with a different or disguised voice. The talk, at first, was mostly mumbling. A figure on my left then started to direct questions to the spirit voice. "Spirit, who are you?" he said.

"You can call me Beau James," the voice replied.

I started to chuckle; a little out of nervousness and also figuring this was going to be a big put-on. I was wondering if they had gotten Jimmy especially for me. I was politely told to be quiet. I recognized the Oracle's voice and hoped I hadn't embarrassed him. I was wondering if this was standard training for morticians. "Spirit, where are you?" the same individual inquired.

"It's not Heaven, baby," the spirit's voice offered.

I had to restrain myself from laughing again. This was beautiful; I didn't know spirits were this hep. We were informed by a member of the circle that it was now an open forum. This meant that anyone could ask a question of the spirit. One figure asked, "Do you know anything about the Knapp Commission?"

"What's the Knapp Commission?" the voice retorted.

"It's investigating police corruption in New York City," the same figure added.

"The New York police are the finest – the finest in everything," the voice chuckled. Hearing the chuckle, I smiled to myself thinking that the medium was probably with the Sanitation Department.

Another figure asked, "What do you think about Mayor Lindsay?"

That's it I said to myself, this is a new type of political rally. "Mayor Lindsay's City Hall is a much hotter place than where I am located," the spirit generously offered. Apparently the mayor had some support in the spirit world. This was getting to be fun. I started to search my mind for a question I could ask.

Another figure asked, "Should I vote for Senator McGovern for President?"

"Vote Republican this year because this place is full of Democrats and we need some more high-ranking Republicans down here," the voice proclaimed.

The spirit must have visited this group before because one of the circle asked, "Have you seen La Guardia lately?"

"Yes, he's still putting out fires. Every time he picks up a comic strip it bursts into flames."

I couldn't think of a good question so I asked, "Who am I?" The voice replied, "Man, you shouldn't ask questions like that – I'm having my own identity crisis."

This caused a few chuckles from a couple of us. I just couldn't imagine a spirit saying that. It sounded more like a blue-collar worker's lament. It went on like that for an hour before the spirit became thirsty and decided to leave.

As we drove back to the Bronx, I told the Oracle that it had been fun, but as far as I was concerned, once was enough. He said to me, "You really didn't believe it, did you?"

"Come on, you're kidding me," I replied. He seemed a little distressed by my answer. I figured I would backtrack as I didn't mean to offend him,, "Those answers did seem pretty funny at the time. I thought it was a charade or something."

He looked at me sternly and said, "Believe me that was no joke; it's for real." I was waiting for him to break into a grin but he never did.

That night I sat down with a map of New York, a Coke, a telephone book, my figures, my observations, a cigar, and my intuition and tried to determine where

I had been. It took me about 40 minutes. It made my night complete.

Two days later he approached me and said, "My group wants to find out if you knew where you were. If you do, we'll have to move."

The Oracle's group was sharper than I had thought. If it hadn't been for an accident of fate they would have easily fooled me. I found out later that they had run sharper men than I, blindfolded, over the same course and they had all come to the same conclusion: Calvary Cemetery in Brooklyn. The accident of fate was that I had moonlighted as a cabbie for four years and had crossed the 59th Street Bridge into Manhattan a thousand times, feeling its highly characteristic grooves and hearing the special sounds of those valleys. It was my favorite and most profitable highflagging trip. I had decided to give Oracle the expected answer and forget the whole thing. "You really want me to tell you?" I replied.

"Yes."

"Okay, we were in an easily recognizable mausoleum in the northeast section of Calvary Cemetery in Brooklyn," I proclaimed.

The Oracle started to laugh but stopped as the anger appeared on my face. Getting control of himself, he added, "Thank you. That was very good. My group wants to thank you for your honesty." He knew he had made a mistake, but he didn't realize the extent of it. I was determined now to find out if my deductions were correct. I was sitting in Horn and Hardart's across from Trinity Church in Manhattan the following Wednesday. At 8:15, I moved toward the church's graveyard. It was completely still, but I didn't see what I had hoped to see. I could have sworn it would be a mausoleum. Everything else fit like a glove – the iron gate, the old leaves, the cool air. I saw a metal door leading into the basement of the church and my hopes rose. As I opened it a crack, I could hear the spirit's voice. I was elated. I opened the door and as the Oracle stared at me, I said, "Oracle, never mock an admirer of Sherlock Holmes," and left. I saw the Oracle two days later and he was all smiles saying, "That was really beautiful." Our relationship has been very professional ever since that day.

Of course much more is experienced by cops when they're off duty. But the good ones never really leave the job. Like Patrolman Creek, they never take their badges off. Sometimes this means justice and sometimes tragedy. I can only marvel at the rare dedication this job frequently elicits from the most unlikely men. I marvel at their ingenuity and deplore a society that gives a man such responsibility and then forces him to take a second job. But that's the nature of things. We get by.

11

As I've mentioned, gangs were suddenly back in style. But now it was no longer fashionable to pass the time on street corners, to lounge on stoops or rooftops. Instead the youths grouped themselves in battalions, usually according to street blocks, and dressed in studded Levi jackets bearing their chosen name; whether it be Ghetto Stompers, or Ghetto Ghouls, or Savage Nomads, the pattern was nearly always the same. They met in the cellars of abandoned tenements or swaggered the streets of their self-declared "turf," much like their compatriots of the fifties. With one exception.

These kids grew up with TV and the ever-present camera eye. They witnessed the civil rights marches, the campus sit-ins, the anti-war protests, the urban riots, and they learned something: how to use that camera. So as the gangs shaped and sharpened themselves, they were also careful to feed the media copy. They existed to clear the streets of pushers and junkies, they said. They were their neighborhoods' last line of defense against crime. Some believed their smooth public relations campaign. In the wake of the upheavals over the Vietnam war and the war on poverty, it became convenient to seek out those who claimed to be "the voice of the people." Frankly, I never met "the people," just a lot of men, women, and children trying to survive against terrible odds. But for a while the gangs held on and fashioned their own forms of terror.

One evening, the Skulls held a war conference in their cellar. They were angry. Several bodegas refused to contribute to the gang's self-improvement fund. The president, a youth named Chico, reportedly told his followers, "We're going to get those motherfuckers." Then he went on, "And while we do that, I want that bastard Ralphie and the pimp Ortiz. They gotta learn this is our turf."

The gang decided to split up into three groups and perform all three missions at the same time. Chico, a sixteen-year-old Venezuelan immigrant, would assault the bodega on Kelly Street; Philo, vice-president of the gang, led his team toward Ralph Gonzalez on Kelly Street; while Dude, a fifteen-year-old, would take on Ortiz.

That night, Angel Fernandez, one of the targets, sold a lot of beer. It was hot, his customers were thirsty. Looking out the front windows of his store he could see only darkness and the lights of an occasional car. Still, he felt good about business and he sent his brother-in-law out to pick up cases from the distributor. Keep pouring it on, summer, he remembers thinking.

So Fernandez was alone when Chico and his comrades approached. Their plan was simple: Burn Fernandez out. For those who don't follow the six o'clock news, the Molotov cocktail, in the proper hands, can be a frighteningly destructive weapon. What makes it even scarier is its simplicity. Just fill a bottle partway with gasoline, stuff the neck with a cork and some cloth soaked with gas, light the gas-soaked cloth, and hurl against the object of your ire. That's what Chico did to Fernandez's bodega.

The bottle shattered against his front window. The gas, both the liquid and the fumes, exploded, shooting flames into the store. Panicked, Fernandez ran toward the front door. That's when Chico sent in his reserves.

While the basic weapon in a gang's arsenal remains the zip gun or the crudest of "Saturday Night Specials," many refinements have been made. Take the one Fernandez faced. It was a flame-thrower made from six empty beer cans taped together. Lit, it shot a six-foot flame of burning gas at Fernandez. Screaming, he retreated to the rear of the store. Satisfied that the bodega was destroyed, Chico and his friends retreated. Neighbors rescued Fernandez, but only after he suffered grievous burns.

In the meantime, Ralph Gonzalez stood on the corner of Kelly Street and Intervale Avenue. He had been expecting an attack eventually. For several months he had tried to organize residents against the gangs, and, as a result, received many threats. His efforts proved useless and now the price would be exacted.

He saw Philo and his followers and turned to flee. It was too late. Shots shattered the silence of the street. One slug ripped his thigh; he felt the cloth of his pants tear before he felt the pain. That's the way it usually is. You're more surprised at first, more outraged that this is happening to you. You don't immediately react to the physical effects. So Gonzalez got up and hopped across Kelly Street. A second bullet whipped his back. As other shots snarled by him, he managed to crawl under an abandoned car.

Unfortunately, the law of the ghetto is not kind to the injured. The windows above the shoot-out quickly filled with laughing observers. A girl leaned out the window and pointed out his refuge. Philo waved thanks, then bent, and emptied his pistol under the car. Ralph was a DOA at Lincoln.

Nobody called us. Someone did pull a fire alarm. A single sector car sped toward the bodega fire.

On Beck Street, José Ortiz stood casually in front of his apartment building. Inside were several of José's girls. José as pimp had not offended the Skulls. What bothered them was that José had recruited one of their own members. They wanted her back along with revenge.

He saw them coming and ran up on the porch of the building. The bullet stopped him on the last step. He fell backwards, splitting his head open as he hit the sidewalk. Satisfied with the blood, the gang left.

When I arrived, there wasn't much more to do. Just another case for the garbage man. Sweep up and move on. In most of these instances, little can be done without help from the community. But for a community to give help, it has to have some positive image of itself, some pride. This community had none. For their indifference, two more statistics would be added to the graph on my office wall. Unfortunately no graph existed for the seriously hurt; there were too many of them.

Sometimes, though, residents of the Four-one prove more resilient than one might expect. They assert their dignity. But often they pay a high price for such foolish expressions of pride.

A family named the Pearls, black, close-knit, moved to the city from North Carolina where the father had been killed in what was described as a hunting accident. There were nine children ranging in age from four to nineteen. After several frustrating months in search of decent housing and jobs, the family went on welfare and was eventually placed in a deteriorating house on Longfellow Avenue. Their drop into welfare and poverty distressed them. The boys found the violence of the street and the politics of the gangs in their neighborhood disturbing; the daughters were repelled by the tough, promiscuous girls.

In turn, the Pearls' aloofness piqued the gangs' pride. They thrived on those that acquiesced. So they beat up a couple of the younger boys. They were in turn warned by the older brothers. The warning only accelerated the beatings. Then, one day, Simon, nineteen, and Butch, seventeen, caught five of the gang torturing nine-year-old Sammy Pearl. They unmercifully beat three of the torturers.

Two of the attackers belonged to the Royal Jades, the third was a visiting member of the Black Devils. We had lists of their activities on the wall. Unfortunately, we didn't know of the fight nor of the meeting that followed in which the beating was reported to the gang leaders. The violence would not be sudden. Rather it would be carefully increased to the point where the Pearls would be forced to toe the line.

That night a rock was thrown through the front door window of the Pearls' home. They made a complaint and a radio car took the report. Rather than seek our protection, the boys decided to defend themselves. Why they made this decision remains a matter of conjecture. Perhaps it was engendered by the circumstances surrounding their father's death. I can't say. But the two eldest boys decided to buy a gun.

Simon had heard some street talk about a candy store that sold Saturday Night Specials. Without friends in the neighborhood, he faced a formidable task. That night, he hit the streets and doggedly set about checking all the candy stores in the area.

Most store owners turned their back on his questions. One said he sold pistols occasionally but had none on hand at the moment. Finally, an owner told him, "Leave your name and address. If I hear anything, I'll get in touch." Simon was excited. "I need 'em in a hurry," he said.

"Friday," the owner said. A price of $25 per weapon was agreed upon.

Late Thursday evening, Mrs. Pearl heard noises at the front door. When she cautiously looked out into the vestibule, she saw four youngsters trying to jimmy the lock of the front door. Her sudden screams drove them away and brought Butch and Simon racing downstairs. Panic grew. They had kept the harassment and the beatings from their mother. Now they knew the situation would only get worse. Although we assigned a patrol car to watch the house, the boys still felt threatened.

Early that morning, they went outside and from the empty lots and tenement cellars they collected bricks, rocks, and bottles, the first-strike capability of the Four-one. These they stored on the porch roof facing the street. Throughout the night, the boys kept their own vigil, staggering sleep periods. Nothing happened.

That morning, Simon returned to the candy store owner. Nothing was said as he handed the money across the counter. In return, the owner showed him an address written on a scrap of paper. Fearing treachery, but fearing gang violence even more, Simon followed the instructions and went to the address. It turned out to be an abandoned building. He walked up three flights of dark and littered stairs that seemed to sway with every step. The dank odor was an unfamiliar scent but he pushed on anyway. The guns were important.

As he shoved open the door he waited for someone to leap on him. Instead the light, uneven and gray, showed a bricked-up fireplace, windowsills torn away, kitchen pipes hanging at odd angles through the ceiling. He found the closet and pulled up a board. A sawed-off shotgun and a .45 caliber automatic lay in the opening. They were loaded.

That night, the family spent the evening eating dinner and watching TV. Neither boy said anything. The danger, they felt, was too enormous for their mother to comprehend. At 10:30, as the summer heat slowly subsided, Eloise, the ten-year-old, excitedly claimed she saw someone in the backyard. Simon and Butch checked but found no one.

About this time, a thirteen-year-old, wearing the Royal Jade colors, strolled into a cellar a short distance away and calmly announced, "It's done. I cut the phone lines." Two others reported that the Molotov cocktails and other weapons were in the positions agreed upon.

Both gangs now worked in concert. They numbered over forty. Orders were issued. Some would attack with long-range missiles from a rooftop across the street. Others planned to assault the porch while the rest would attack the rear. At 10:45, the assault groups moved out.

Twelve Jades and Devils charged the front porch and started to knock out all the windows with pipes and bats. Down came the front door. The door in the rear gave way to a strong assault. Two squads in the street peppered the house with bricks and rocks which had been neatly concealed in the Pearls' own garbage cans.

As the family realized the phone was dead, a squad from the gang broke through to the vestibule. Simon and Butch gathered the children together and then Simon raced upstairs for the weapons. One firebomb landed on the porch. A second set fire to the front of the house. Simon returned downstairs as the main attack hit the front door. He fired two blasts from his shotgun. The blasts shook the building, flashing in the dark confined space, and made the children cry. Several of the attackers, wounded, retreated. That gave the two boys time to hustle the mother, the grandmother, and kids upstairs. Thick, oily flames lapped at the living room. As Simon tried to beat them back, the cellar door slowly opened. He didn't pause to measure the consequences of his reaction; he grabbed the shotgun and let go with two blasts. Then he retreated upstairs.

By this time, the rest of the family was terrified and screaming unrestrainedly. Looking out the window, both Simon and Butch realized they were surrounded with no immediate help in sight. Time, they knew, favored the attackers. The flames slowly spread.

Simon had not lost his sense of command. He gave Butch the shotgun and ordered him to the front bedroom windows. With the .45 he guarded the stairs. They waited. Simon admitted later that his legs shook so much he had to kneel and prop his body against the wall.

Several shotgun blasts came from the front room. Butch had spotted firebombers on the roof across the street. The pellets from his gun hit a young boy who had been at his window watching the action. Irate, the mother called us. It was our first report of the siege and it took the injury of a child, whose mother would otherwise have been unconcerned, to alert us. "What the hell do they think this is, TV?" I said to Moe when it was all over.

By that time, eleven attackers were in the living room, fanning the fire. Several gang members crouched at the foot of the darkened stairs. They held .25 caliber pistols and exchanged shots with Simon. As a shoot-out, it was a sloppy affair. Chips of wood and plaster from the walls and ceiling rained on the stairs. The two boys upstairs remained determined in their effort to hold what little ground remained to them.

They were still blasting away when we reached the scene. I sent one unit around to the back of the building and we breached the front door. We managed to nab seven of the gang. As we brought the children and their guardians out of the house, the Fire Department arrived. "Sorry," I told my lieutenant "friend" from the Fox Street fire, "no fun left. All the windows are broken." He didn't even smile.

After the fire was out, the family returned to their home. They refused to go to a welfare hotel. When they first arrived in the city, they had spent a couple of months in one. Their fourteen-year-old girl was raped during that stay. I stationed a radio car in front of the house until the family could be relocated. Nobody went to jail. I got the feeling the courts thought it was just a group of kids playing Cowboys and Indians.

One particular night, I remember, the heat lay on us like a blanket and tempers were short. We expected trouble. The Youth Division warned us about a possible battle between the Ghetto Ghouls and the Savage Skins in the Bryant Avenue-Westchester Avenue vicinity. I assigned Patrolmen McCoy and Velez to the area. Jim McCoy was an enthusiastic and highly competent officer who took his job very seriously while Velez was a fairly sluggish man who, despite his excellent sense of humor, was always in trouble. I still felt his talents complemented McCoy's and wanted to see how they worked out as a team.

Moe and I had just swept up the final details of a homicide over in Hunts Point when McCoy came on the radio. "There're about fifty kids in small groups walking south on Westchester toward Southern Boulevard," he said. Several cars told Central they were on the way and we joined them.

McCoy was right. The Skins were trying to slip out of their territory in small groups to rumble with the Ghouls. They were slowly coming together and were marching toward Simpson Street. I asked Central for five cars to turn them back there. Then we heard shots.

I could hear McCoy yelling, "There's a guy down on the southeast corner of Simpson. Another guy's running east. He's got a gun. I'm going after him." Moe slammed his foot on the gas. The more cars there, maybe the less shooting there would be.

Whoever choreographed the action must have possessed an absurdly surreal vision of life, or else he saw the Four-one with unusual clarity. McCoy exchanged shots with the man as Velez wheeled the car.

"Central," McCoy was yelling now. "Have a car hit 163rd Street and Simpson. He's heading that way."

"Did someone check the guy down?" I asked.

"Yeah. He's dead, Lou," said an anonymous voice.

"Is he a gang member?"

"No. Male, Puerto Rican, about forty," was the answer.

McCoy continued his pursuit on foot. It led to a dilapidated building further along Simpson. Some women standing in front of the building pleaded with us not to shoot and, since we weren't receiving any fire, we held off. More people are shot by stray bullets in this area than by shots aimed at actual targets.

Velez went up the adjoining building as Moe and I followed McCoy. Several more shots erupted further up the staircase. Nearing the roof, we saw McCoy lying in a doorway, gasping violently for air. A man stood above him. As we approached, he raised his hands, the fight apparently out of him.

I called for assistance and Moe lifted McCoy and carried him downstairs. Back-up units arrived and took the prisoner to the precinct. We headed the other way and got McCoy to Jacobi Hospital in the north Bronx in seven minutes.

As the doctors examined McCoy, he regained consciousness. "I was chasing this guy upstairs," he said. "I fired three times and he threw his gun out the window. I think it was from the third floor. He stood on the roof with his hands up. When I reached him and started to go for my handcuffs, bingo, I blacked out. He didn't touch me."

McCoy's explanation seemed explicit enough: a combination of the intense heat, physical exertion, and emotional pressure felled him. It happens to any guy and McCoy was lucky the man he pursued offered no resistance. Still, McCoy was a popular officer and I knew that if word got around he was in the hospital after a chase, the men would steam. So I told them over the radio that he dropped from heat exhaustion. Things remained calm.

As it turned out, a simple robbery inadvertently solved our temporary gang problem. Believing they were being fired upon, the gangs retreated. They were quiet for the rest of the night. Unquestionably they would return, with their chains, their sticks, their pistols. These kids weren't going anywhere and they knew it. So, like mangy dogs, they ran together in packs, preyed on one another, and exhausted themselves trying to find a way out. It is a tragedy both for them and their victims.

12

A COP GOT KILLED in the Four-one last night. Another cop, with him, could have been killed. The thought scares me. Normally I work and sleep and work with relative ease. I like to think that I can master most situations. It's the sense that I will prevail that has gotten me through some pretty tough spots. But that doesn't mean my hands haven't shaken, my legs haven't felt weak. It could always happen to you.

Here's what happened. A thirteen-year-old Puerto Rican boy was kidnapped from Fox Street at gunpoint and taken to an apartment. The boy, stunned by the sexual depravity of his captor, saw an opportunity and fought his way out of the apartment. There was no help beneath the pale street lights. What few people were in evidence seemed alien, gathered in tight knots around bars and at the counters of bodegas. Finally he reached the Four-one.

Told with any sensitivity, his story remains a strong one, one of assault, senseless attack, helplessness, pain, humiliation. Once the story was out, the detectives moved. Using a description of the building where he had been held, they quickly arrived at the scene. The accused man, Alonzo Simmons, was just getting into his car. He accepted his arrest quite placidly and was taken to the station house. For once the streets lay still; no protests were raised.

Maybe it was his demeanor, his appearance, but the arresting officers got sloppy. Detectives Milo and Banner, having made the arrest, were at their desks completing the paperwork. A third detective, Joe Pitch, fingerprinted the subject. A relatively simple procedure, fingerprinting does require the officer to stand close to the subject. The correct procedure is to remove or unload one's weapon. Usually, you shield your gun with your body as you take his or her fingers, ink them, and roll them over the criminal identification form. Pitch must have had a lapse. Simmons leaped at him, gabbing at Joe's gun. A stool shattered and a table got knocked into the wall during the struggle. Pitch managed to get possession of his revolver, but Simmons knocked it to the floor. Milo and Banner ducked behind their desks as the prisoner came up with the gun. Two explosions brightened the squad room. Pitch fell, clutching his gut.

Another detective, named Lash, working in an adjoining office, heard the commotion, then the shots. As he charged into the room, he met Simmons. For a fraction of a second, they faced one another. Simmons fired his pistol; Lash returned the fire. Simmons fell back against the wall and then collapsed like a drunk suddenly losing control of his legs. He was dead. None of his bullets touched Lash.

When the detectives rolled Pitch over, they could see he too was dead. One shot had shattered his chest, the other tore into his stomach. They were stunned. One minute alive, going about his work, liked by some, derided by others. Now he lay dead. He was the second of ten policemen to die on duty that year.

Policemen mourn such losses publicly. The only other time we get noticed by the law-abiding public is when we hand out a traffic ticket. But this isn't sour grapes. The death of another cop offers intimations of your own mortality and you tremble a bit more.

So you wear your best uniform and you stand in a sharp blue line. You hoist the heavy coffin, covered with black crepe, and bear the contents toward a narrow hole in the ground. And then when you stand up, you realize that half your prayers were made for yourself. For it is only when you stand in that long blue line, outside some chapel you probably never saw before and hope to God you'll never see again, living or dead, that you realize how alone you are.

You also remember as the rain beats down (for some reason it always rains those days) those that died and those that nearly did. The subsequent litany is depressing but necessary.

There's a patrolman named Wonder, and one afternoon he met Sidney Frankel. For over thirty years Frankel operated a hardware store on Hunts Point Avenue. He had witnessed the area's precipitous decline, yet he hung on. Why I don't know. Memories, perhaps. It could be that rents were low, or other competition had quit the neighborhood. But he was concerned about the crime rate and for several months petitioned the Department about getting a foot patrolman for the area.

When Sid went out for lunch, Wonder had already passed the store and his presence made Frankel feel comfortable. He headed for the luncheonette on the corner. The day was bright, and behind him, toward the Sound, the sky was a gaudy July blue. As Frankel turned from this view, he saw Wonder stumble out of the front door of the building.

At about this time Moe and I were cruising through the sidestreets moving away from Hunts Point Avenue. We were talking about our vacation plans. Moe was saving a couple of weeks for the

185

hunting season, but figured that he and his wife, Beverly, would probably get away for a weekend alone. My wife had made plans to spend some time on Cape Cod as she wanted to visit the Irish Wailing Wall, the stockade fence surrounding the Kennedy compound.

The sight baffled Frankel. The patrolman staggered, fell onto the sidewalk, struggled up again only to fall by the curb. Then Frankel noticed the knife sticking out of the man's back. He promptly ran to the nearest store and called 911; a 10-13 was broadcast.

By that time, Moe and I were at the other end of the precinct. I quickly checked my roll and verified that the post was covered by a foot patrolman. Moe, as usual a compendium of useful information, filled me in as we headed for the scene. Wonder, he said, was aggressive and competent. He had seen a lot of action and was highly decorated. By the time we got there an ambulance had come and gone, hopefully in time. I set up a temporary headquarters in Frankel's store and started piecing the story together.

According to witnesses. Wonder had seen two men peering down from the roof. He decided to investigate. Given his record it was easy to understand. He scrambled up the six flights. When he reached the roof, it seemed empty.

You have to understand that an empty roof is not really an empty roof. First there is the exit, usually a small, square structure that initially blocks your view of the entire surface. Sometimes there are ventilators and, if the building is big enough, a water tower. So Wonder had a lot to think about when he hit the roof.

They struck him as he emerged from the stairs. One rushed at him while the second plunged a knife into his back. Only his screams apparently drove them off. He lay on the hot tar of the roof for a while as the blood trickled out. Then he got up and staggered slowly down stairs. On his way to the street, he pounded on several doors; no one responded. It's that kind of precinct. St. Francis of Assisi, complete with a display kit of home-grown pigeons, couldn't get a door to open there. How he made it should be published in the AMA *Journal*, but it won't be. Just another case of survival in the Four-one. Several months later, Wonder resumed his beat.

"Shots fired," the radio blurted. "Vyse and 172nd Street." Central then sent a description. Bill Milo and his partner Jim Banner sped to the scene. They caught a glimpse of the man described as he entered a building. Milo pursued him through the door and up the stairs. As he entered the hallway, Milo met the man. And the man held a .38 caliber Iver Johnson revolver. He jammed it into Milo's chest and pulled the trigger. The silence was almost as frightening as the anticipated explosion. The gun simply clicked. Milo almost fainted but had the presence of mind to draw his own gun and fire. The suspect fell dead; his weapon still had two live rounds in it. To this day, Milo cannot remember what passed through his brain during that awful second.

Over the past fifteen years, the city has slowly made the Hunts Point Market the center for wholesale fruit and vegetable sales. It's still being expanded. An enormous amount of money passes from one hand to another there. Translation: The area needs heavy police protection. We try. But the area covers more than a dozen acres, has over a hundred warehouses, and many railroad sidings where freight cars stand waiting to be unloaded. Because of its size, complexity, and the money exchanged, it attracts many criminals, burglars, gamblers, drug pushers, addicts, and prostitutes. No wonder a large number of our calls came from this area.

Assigned exclusively to the area was Sector Thomas. Two patrolmen walk the docks during business hours and one man is assigned to the booth area. The quietest post of all was down by the water, down a dirt road from the booth area. There an officer occupied an abandoned school bus guarding vouchered automobiles. Called "the student's post," a man could sit and read without distraction. The only problem was the mosquitoes. One rumor, never confirmed, held that an older officer never performed the act of love better than in that old school bus. His fervor, it went on, was spurred by those mosquitoes feeding on his bare buttocks.

This particular night, a patrolman named Shaw manned the booth. Patrolmen Karris and Totter covered in Sector Thomas while a man named Kenya had the pound. Compared with the rest of the precinct this place, at night, was considered peaceful. Occasional prostitution or attempts at pilfering were the major criminal activities. So it was not unusual when Sector Thomas got called out of the market area to assist another unit.

As they left, an old man approached Shaw in the booth. Some men were breaking into a train, he said and gave directions. Shaw figured it was probably some bums since the place drew them like roaches. He felt no fear and in fact welcomed the action.

He walked down several rows of parked freight cars before he saw two men standing beside an empty door. They appeared docile enough as he approached. Then one of the men waved. It was too late. A third man leaped out of the shadows and plunged a hunting knife into Shaw's back. Later he remembered thinking, "Shit, I'm gone, I'm gone now." He fell, tried to get up but couldn't. The small sharp stones of the roadbed cut into his chest and he thought that it was a helluva place to die. As if to make it worse, the three men gathered over his prostrate body and kicked him. Then, figuring he was dead, they fled.

Shaw was almost but not quite gone. He clutched his walkie-talkie and called in a 10-13. Kenya, in the bus, heard him. So did several sector cars.

"Where the hell are you?" one of them called.

"In back. Near the trains," he called.

The cars screamed through, the gate and headed in that direction. They couldn't find him. More cars joined the search. What they didn't know was that Shaw was unfamiliar with the area. Calls kept going out, trying to calm him, trying to get a more accurate description of his surroundings. All the while, Shaw's voice grew weaker. Emergency service, detectives, TPF, and about ten Four-one units combed the area.

What none of us realized was that Shaw, in his ignorance of the area, kept telling us he was "in the back"; he was really in the front. The frustration had reached an awful pitch when we heard Kenya screaming, "We've found him, we've found him." They rushed him to the hospital where he was listed in serious condition. One of the knife thrusts had reached the kidney area and although he will survive, the wound was such that, chances are, his days as a cop are over.

*

One night, Patrolman Marsh and his newly assigned partner, John Kramer, in Sector John, were sent to a building on the 1100 block on Simpson Street. It sounded like a family fight.

The building was one of the better ones in the area. That is to say, there were no burned-out apartments, the stairs seemed solid, and there was light in the halls. There might have been rats and roaches, but after several months in the Four-one, they became part of the landscape.

The call came from a fifth floor apartment, and the two men sweated heavily as they made their way up. "This is the third job in a row," Marsh complained, "on the fifth floor. You know we don't have one elevator in our sector. I wish they would tear it all down and put up a project. At least projects have elevators."

They reached the apartment and took turns punching the bell and slugging the door. Finally a diminutive elderly lady opened it. She was very calm as she invited the men into the front room. As bottles were thrown, furniture crashed, voices screamed, she explained this rather delicate family dispute.

Apparently her daughter, already on welfare, expected her boyfriend and she was trying to get her drunken husband out of the apartment. Others got into the act. Another woman and her boyfriend also argued with the drunk. As Marsh and his partner waded in they learned that the basic question being discussed was who was going to party with the group, the husband or the boyfriend? After listening to five minutes of clamorous calumny, Marsh asked the husband to step downstairs. Since it was the wife's apartment, and welfare paid the rent on the basis that the husband had deserted her, he had no legal right to be there. And she wanted him out.

But he refused to budge and things heated up. When the two groups began pushing and shoving, the rookie called in a 10-13. Marsh tried to separate them, which angered all concerned. They turned on him. The three men pounded him to the floor. When Kramer tried to reenter the room, the three women attacked him. Marsh was being unmercifully beaten when the responding unit knocked down the door. They were followed by another unit and together they did a job on the three men. Marsh lay still, his face already swollen, his arm broken. Infuriated by the sight of him lying on the floor, the officers evened the score. I'm not condoning their action. But sometimes you get so pissed off you can't help it. I know we're paid to keep our tempers in check, but on the other hand you can't allow precedents. Word gets around and the next thing you know cops are being stomped on street corners. Anyway, the boyfriend showed up an hour later and found the apartment turned upside down and empty, except for the grandmother.

Then there are those agonizing moments that you have to live with for years after, when one officer mistakenly wounds another. This, sadly, is a classic case.

A man named Bell opened the door to his apartment and immediately two men jumped him. Fists struck him on the head and around the kidneys; his vision took on a reddish tint, he gasped for breath. They grabbed at his clothes and told him in hoarse tones to disrobe. He complied. They shoved him to the floor and made him lie there while they ransacked his apartment. Then they fled. Another Four-one robbery had been completed using a typical method of operation. Bell called us.

Three detectives were assigned to the case. In many similar instances mental anguish takes a greater toll than physical injury or loss. Bell was very cooperative and he had a good memory. One of the detectives was a man named Lark, a bright and canny man. After Bell's description, he and his partners had a pretty good idea of who they were looking for and where they could be found.

They spotted the alleged robbers the next day on Hoe Avenue. Unfortunately the pair knew Lark as well as he knew them. They fled. Stopping behind a stoop and some garbage cans, they drew revolvers and opened fire. The detectives returned the fire. People scattered, then made for their windows to watch a little drama that for a while would surpass "As the World Turns" or "The Edge of Night."

The two men realized they were outgunned and fled into a partially abandoned building. Lark quickly sent a man around to the rear and then raced up the stairs. They cornered their prey on the fourth floor, in a vacant apartment. The hall was narrow, and the doorway presented such an angle that no direct fire could be directed against it. He went downstairs and called for assistance. That assistance included "the Hammer."

In police parlance, "the Hammer" is known as "the Key." It's what you use to get by objects that are placed there to prevent you from doing so. "The Hammer" had a great track record when it came to getting by obstacles. It was a huge and heavy sledge-hammer that had originally been purchased in the twenties to deal with speakeasies. It then moved to Harlem in the thirties where it interrupted the business operations of numerous gambling and after-hours joints. Then it was sent to the Village where apparently it had second thoughts about the dubiousness of some public morals laws. Its alcohol-soaked handle cracked as it broke down the door of a gay club.

The officer then in charge had three choices (1) He could send it to the Police Museum; (2) send it to Father Dunne's alcoholic counseling office, or (3) he could cover up its weaknesses and try to nurse it back to health himself. So in its old age, "the Hammer" found itself in the relatively placid Five-o precinct which covers the sylvan expanses of the North Bronx. But then the Department had second thoughts about it being in an area where the citizens were so law-abiding and it got shipped to the Four-one. It was a lousy way to treat such an old and trustworthy performer.

"The Hammer" rose to the occasion. Two quick blows by a muscular patrolman and the door shattered. Shots barked on the roof. The two men had fled down the fire escape. Sending his other men out the window after them, Lark hustled down the stairs.

By then every window on the street framed at least one grinning face. This was better than "Hawaii Five-O," especially for those that didn't have color TV's. Two latecomers, Patrolman Kowalski and his partner, "the Bird," split up; the Bird went to the rear of the building while Kowalski went through the front door.

He came face to face with a young black male holding a gun. Kowalski stiffened. "Hold it," he yelled. The other man stared at him. Kowalski thought he detected a movement, it might have been very slight, no more than a twitch. You are taught not to gamble with subjective judgments at such times and the Patrolman fired. The bullet struck Lark in the left side, partially spun him around, and flung him back against the stairs. He didn't have time to pull out his badge.

Luckily Lark recovered, but the tragedy lingers on. You'd like to say it was an honest mistake, one committed in the midst of some very tense action. Clearly, judgment is impossible. Was Kowalski quicker on the trigger because the man facing him was black? Did Lark freeze because of some latent loathing of the police although he himself was now one of them? I must reject any simple answers. So I responded by insisting that regulations be followed – that the nonuniformed officer have his badge pinned on his shirt or jacket when he went into an action, that he obey all instructions from a uniformed officer until his identity is established, and, though I regret that we have to do this, Central should advise all units responding to a call that black, nonuniformed officers are also on the scene. At the same time uniformed officers, black and white, should maintain discipline.

One of the suspects was caught going down the fire escape. The second got away, but not for long. Two days later he was found on the steps of a Southern Boulevard apartment house, dead from an overdose.

My last example of the extra price police frequently pay while on the job involved a man named Charlie Jones. By any definition of the word, he was a decent man. Recently married, he held a steady job and lived, by Four-one standards at least, in a nice apartment. A man, many would say, who had a great deal to look forward to.

One night he got back from work to find his wife in tears. Burglars had emptied half their apartment. Jones recognized the M.O. immediately. He also knew that in all probability neighborhood junkies were responsible. They would select a victim and then monitor his work habits. If the wife worked, as Mrs. Jones did, all the better. If the apartment was a rear one, as the Joneses' was, better yet. Then, while the husband and wife were out, they would systematically loot the place. Often it took them more than one day to remove all the belongings. To Jones, this meant they would be back.

Finesse and skill are two words unknown in the Four-one. Events buffeted a resident brutally and directly. So Charlie went to his bottom bureau drawer and took out an illegally acquired revolver. Once again events were sent into motion; they would leave one man dead and another unable to work again. When I eventually collected the details I found myself calling the South Bronx a necropolis. It was a city of death.

Jones spent the next morning and early afternoon nervously. By habit, he was not a man of violence. A steady job, a hot meal, a warm bed beside his wife dominated his dreams. Others had different visions. At 1:40 P.M. the junkies began their assault. A neighbor who heard them called the precinct. Patrolmen Anger and Fry, both in plainclothes, headed for the address.

The attack came from two directions. Several men worked on the bedroom window while one banged away at yesterday's weak spot, the door. Charlie's wife became hysterical and sat screaming in a corner of the bedroom. Charlie stationed himself by the bedroom door. That position gave him a clear line of sight to both the rear windows and the front door.

By this time, other units were responding. Anger and Fry arrived and ran up the stairs. The man at the door, hearing them, raced to the roof. Those at the window also retreated. Charlie stood alone in his darkened apartment as the pummeling stopped and the door slowly opened. He saw two shabbily dressed men enter and begin to probe their way through the apartment toward him. The only noise was the steady sobbing of his wife.

The two men heard a gun cock and saw Charlie at the same time. No words crossed the dark room, just bullets. They stood fifteen feet apart. Sixteen shots were fired. Jones fell into the doorway, torn by several of the eleven bullets pumped at him. Anger fell across a sofa, five bullets in him, grievously wounded. We rushed him to Jacobi Hospital where nearly one hundred policemen came to give blood. He survived but he'll never walk a beat again.

13

I HATED TO LEAVE the Four-one. I had earned a promotion and that meant an automatic transfer to another precinct. In this instance it would be the relatively quiet Five-O.

Serving in the Four-one has made me realize how fortunate I am to be a cop. As a moderately talented physicist, how many people could I have helped? Whereas here, I saw daily people whose names and addresses are long forgotten, but whose acknowledging smiles sparked a sense of warmth that made me know it has been worthwhile. The wrinkled, old black lady whose cardiac husband we saved one morning, smiling and waving from her second floor window; the militant black father's self-conscious smile for us as we passed, for saving his knife-punctured son; the young Puerto Rican girl's shy smile, for interrupting and capturing her unsuccessful rapist; the comely white woman's broad smile, as she entered the supermarket with her stroller, for saving her gagging baby; the grateful shoe store owner, whose attackers we captured, waving enthusiastically as Moe slowed to return the courtesy. I feel that I have been a success. I think that Moe and I have made a contribution.

Looking back, I realize there are some people you can't get through to, enter an intelligent discussion with, or even get a smile from. They feed on hate and let it dictate the course of their lives. It was all a great rollercoaster ride that veered between love and hate, spinning the world by so quickly you never knew where to get off.

When I was with Moe I sensed this feeling of mutual admiration. It was an admiration based on the fact that we did the job in the best and most humane way. We tried like hell to be civil; most of the time we were successful. When we weren't, we took a stand and backed each other up.

When I came to the Four-one, I wanted to become a good cop. I now realize that a good cop is a decent human being with the guts to be decent under trying circumstances. It had been there all the time.

When fellow officers would tell me that my father was a tough but fair boss, I would respond, "I don't know what kind of cop he was, but he was a good father." I now realize that he was a good father for the same reason he was a good cop; he was strict but fair. It had been there all the time. The Four-one Precinct has helped me to reach maturity; it was horrible, it was poignant, it was funny, it was sad, but most of all it was real.

Most people look for simple answers. Cops are the same way. After working in a place like this you realize there are no easy answers. The best thing is to "give a damn" and then go out and try to do something about it. It reminded me of what a friend had once told me, "Good thoughts are fine, but if the thoughts don't activate good works, those thoughts ain't worth a damn."

Other memories drifted back to me during those last few days.

A 10-20 came over the radio. The location was Intervale and Fox. Moe shook his head in despair. "Probably Cora's bodega again," he said. "She's been hit hard recently." We rolled. Cora was a special friend.

This time she did get hit hard. Her husband lay dead on the floor. She was hysterical as we entered and fell into Moe's arms. Eventually we got the story out of her.

Cora was in the back of the store when the robber entered. She heard his demand and saw him pull out his gun. So she grabbed a kitchen knife and attacked him. Unfortunately, she would have been more effective if she still had her "$1,000 pistol." As she charged down the narrow aisle, the man easily ducked and flung her to the floor. Cora's husband made his move and the man brought the weapon back up. This time he pulled the trigger. The shot from the .45 must have sounded like a gas main going off. The bullet drilled Cora's husband between his eyes and left half of his brain splashed across a shelf full of Spaghetti-O's.

After all this, we figured Cora would return to Puerto Rico. She didn't. Her store remains open in a very dangerous area. Every time I was in the neighborhood, I made it a point to stop by and say hello. The Four-one has a lot of people like Cora and needs many more.

————————

A black cop came in one day and handed in his resignation. I sat stunned at my desk, looking at the official form, unable to believe what I read. He stood there, a muscular, handsome man with a fine record.

I had always found him to be very articulate and pleasant.

His name was Richie Hyde and he had been on the force four years and all of his active time was spent in the Four-one. He was returning to Atlanta, he said, to work in the family business, which wouldn't pay all that well but which involved a lot fewer hassles. I suspect he was angered over the Department's failure to rotate him out of the Four-one. There were a lot of young guys in the same boat. The old-timers would get the first shot at getting out. It was only fair. Whatever the reason, we were about to lose a helluva cop.

He asked me what I thought of his decision. I told him that from what he said it was personal. He agreed. My mind twisted in knots and I still couldn't find the words to ask him to withdraw the application. Later, I asked myself why it was possible that a black man would rather work in Atlanta than be a cop here. "How bad off is the city," I asked myself, "when a black man would want to return to Georgia to get away from it?" I winced inwardly for I knew the answer.

Sergeant Grit finally got fed up with Hector Ruiz, the bounty hunter. He ordered him to stop hanging around the precinct house and threatened to throw Ruiz out. Ruiz, a historical figure at the Fort, stood his ground as any landmark should. Grit ordered the Polack to arrest him. Reluctantly, since Ruiz was a friend of long standing, the Polack agreed.

At Ruiz's trial for disorderly conduct, the Polack testified in expert fashion. After his many years of service, he had polished his courtroom techniques brightly. He sat in awe of few defense attorneys, and since Ruiz defended himself, he didn't sweat a bit. The judge fined Ruiz $25.

Relieved, Ruiz reached for his wallet. Then he stared with shock at the contents. Not enough in there to pay the fine. "Hey, Polack," he yelled. "You owe me $25 from that Mets game last week." The Polack stopped short. He knew Ruiz was correct and he would have liked to continue on his way, but that would run counter to accepted Four-one ethics. "Always pay your ticket when it becomes due," it read somewhere.

So an astonished judge looked on as a convicted criminal and his principal accuser exchanged money. The Polack didn't have the full amount but together they came up with the fine. "What the hell is going on here?" the judge roared.

"I dunno," the Polack said. "But can't a cop have a friend?"

One night we found a girl nude and unconscious, lying beside a burning truck. The officers, seeing that she was badly burned, rushed her to Lincoln Hospital. There her leg had to be amputated.

Returning to investigate, the officers found some of her clothes and her wallet. She was a fourteen-year-old girl who lived on Fox Street. When she regained consciousness, she told us her story.

Walking home from a girl friend's home, she was grabbed by two boys and forced into the abandoned truck. The act seemed spontaneous and this heightened its viciousness. They beat and raped her repeatedly. Then they tied her up and started the fire. Luckily she had gotten a good look at one of the boys and gave us a positive identification.

We turned the case over to the detectives. Within an hour the suspects were brought in. I looked at Mac, our community relations man, when I saw who one of them was. It was Claude Howard's son again, one of the two who had thrown the Martinez boy from the roof a couple of months before. I felt no happiness, only relief. If the charges were true then two animals had been swept off the street.

I said to Mac, "At least you saved one of those kids on your program." He shook his head. He wasn't listening. He wasn't thinking about the one he saved but about the one he lost.

True to form, Mr. Howard stormed into the station demanding his son's release. Justice hasn't served any of us very well, I thought. The Howards, the police, the girl. She'd been used heinously. We earned an inimical hatred and a father's prejudices were only reinforced. And in all probability the boy will shortly return to the streets where he will repeat his crimes. The strength of my men sometimes becomes a marvel to me.

———————

The boys would miss Sid at the station house; he had given his last history lesson on the precinct.

Once it had been a famous synagogue. When I attended Sid's funeral service I found only a rabbi and two elderly people. Sid who was so full of life, seemed abandoned in death. I hoped for something better. I like to think I'm a man not easily moved by cheap emotion. It takes an occasion such as the people standing on the railroad platform, singing the "Battle Hymn of the Republic" as the train bearing Robert F.

Kennedy passed, to really move me. On the scale of things, I thought Sid deserved similar attention in the Four-one. As it was, we could only embrace our private griefs.

I met Sid's two remaining relatives. They told me how they had tried to get him to move to the North Bronx and how he insisted on remaining here, on his beloved Fox Street. They told me his life had been full and happy and that such a life was its own reward. He lived and died as he chose, they said, and a man cannot ask for more than that. As I left, it sank in: We have no right to feel sorry for a man who possesses so strong a heart, so bright a spirit. That was Sid.

From Sid's world to the Fort Apache of the early seventies was a jump not only in time but in consciousness. The old Irish and Jewish population was dispersed and we were caught up in a swelling tide of black and Puerto Rican self-consciousness. One incident illuminates this fact.

Forty agitated, disgruntled Puerto Ricans blocked the school door as if they had taken instructions from Vince Lombardi. Thirty patient blacks waited calmly to enter the school with the newly elected principal who was also black. The police, all twelve of us, stood between the menacing forces. It was an old, old play that we had participated in many times.

In this instance we checked and found that the blacks had the right to enter the school under a mandate laid down by a recent election. I asked them to stay back while we handled things. "Handling things" meant, after several hours of unrelenting argument, forming a wedge and driving at the doors. Little blood flowed, and the door was secured.

The Puerto Ricans had fought courageously, but with honesty. They believed they needed more voice in the school administration and perhaps they were right. At the same time, they were not vicious, and we reciprocated.

One might figure the blacks and Puerto Ricans to be natural political allies. But this is not the case in the Four-one. This area is a battleground for control of the schools, the poverty programs, and political patronage. In this instance, I feel, they are no different than any other immigrant groups. From the sidelines I watched with a degree of pride as they tried to forge some sort of destiny. As long as that destiny did not mean violence.

I saw them as tackling a frontier different from the ones my great-grandfather and his relatives faced when they came to this country from Ireland, just before the civil war. But these new immigrants face another wilderness and I cannot begrudge them their efforts to find a place in society. I only ask that they respect our earnest efforts to keep that frontier peaceful.

When I left the Fort, Moe decided to go back to a sector car. He had had enough of driving bosses. My move to the Five-O meant a jump back. It was peaceful; its streets wound around the hills that make the Hudson so beautiful and, in the summer, trees shrouded the sidewalk with cool shade. I left the South Bronx I had come to love, the Bronx of many textured faces, streets swollen with life, throbbing with voices, change jangling in pockets, shoes moving to the next exciting block.

The last time I saw the Four-one, few people recognized me. I did not find that fact troublesome. I rested easily in my guise as policeman. And I felt there was nothing in the past at the Four-one that should cause me foreboding. My job was done in this special hell.

I simply came back to pick up my last paycheck. Parking was still tough, but I managed to find a spot near the station house. As in the past two summers, the heat lay everywhere and only the young showed signs of energy as they romped through open hydrants. I dodged them and the cars that stood on stilts made of metal milk crates. Rust seemed to be the only timepiece suited for this neighborhood – rust and occasional blotches of blood. I tried but I could not ignore Simpson Street.

Across from the Fort, a small group of excited people gathered. They lacked the boisterousness that marked many crowds. A patrolman named Bill Smyth stood among them, unthreatened. In the center of the crowd lay a three-year-old boy. He had apparently fallen from a fifth floor window and been impaled on the prongs of a wrought iron fence. When I arrived, he still struggled to free himself, but it was too late.

How it happened, no one will know. Faces always lined these windows, watching the precinct. I had probably seen this kid a hundred times, I thought, as Bill Smyth and the ambulance attendant carefully extricated him and placed him on a stretcher. I stood there, taller than most of the crowd. The sun reddened my complexion, and didn't tan it. I was very separate from these people. Yet, after these two years, I sensed we were very much the same. But I could take that one step back. Most of them would never be given a similar chance.

I went into the precinct house and collected my last check. Good-byes. All around me were good-byes.

Then I walked back into the street and the sun and the sound of people. When I got into my car, I paused for a moment. And then I thought of that child who smiled so readily, who sought the same sun and heard the same voices, and felt the wetness on my cheek. I couldn't remember the last time I had cried. I hoped no one would see me. For a moment, I sat and listened to the street, knowing I would always hear it, and then I turned over the ignition and drove away.

Gould Publications

New York Price List and Order Form

• (Effective June 21, 2000) •

☐ New York Alcoholic Beverage Control Law [Softcover] (ISBN 0-87526-377-1)	$ 6.00
☐ New York Banking Law (ISBN 0-87526-235-X)	$ 59.00
☐ New York City Building Code (ISBN 0-87526-128-0)	$ 49.95
☐ New York City Building Code on CD-ROM (ISBN 0-87526-511-1)	$ 99.00*
☐ New York City Fire Law Handbook (ISBN 0-87526-335-6)	$ 19.95
☐ New York City Housing Maintenance Code (ISBN 0-87526-278-3)	$ 19.95
☐ New York City Law Digest (ISBN 0-87526-302-X)	$ 15.95
☐ New York City Police Department (N.Y.P.D.) Patrol Guide Manual [Softcover] (ISBN 0-87526-556-1)	$ 29.95
☐ New York City Police Department (N.Y.P.D.) Patrol Guide DiskLaw™ on CD-ROM (ISBN 0-87526-498-0)	$ 49.95**
☐ New York City Traffic Rules [Looseleaf insert] (ISBN 0-87526-329-1)	$ 6.95
☐ New York Civil Practice Law & Rules DiskLaw™ on CD-ROM (ISBN 0-87526-463-8)	$ 49.95*
☐ New York Civil Practice Law & Rules Handbook [Softcover or Looseleaf] (ISBN 0-87526-390-9)	$ 21.95
☐ New York Civil Service Law (ISBN 0-87526-363-1)	$ 9.95
☐ New York Consolidated Laws [9-volume set] [Softcover or Looseleaf]	$ 179.00
☐ New York Consolidated Laws Unannotated (NYCU™) on CD-ROM	$ 179.00
☐ New York Consolidated Laws Legal Assistant Edition (ISBN 0-87526-360-2)	$ 49.95
☐ New York Corporation Law DiskLaw™ on CD-ROM (ISBN 0-87526-465-4)	$ 49.95*
☐ New York Corporation Law Handbook [Softcover or Looseleaf] (ISBN 0-87526-330-5)	$ 24.95
☐ New York Correction Law Handbook (ISBN 0-87526-403-4)	$ 12.95
☐ New York Court Forms (ISBN 0-87526-250-3)	$ 39.95
☐ New York Courts Manual of Procedure (ISBN 0-87526-180-9)	$ 34.95
☐ New York Criminal and Civil Forfeitures by *Steven L. Kessler* [Softcover or Looseleaf] (ISBN 0-87526-543-X)	$ 44.95
☐ New York *Canudo* on Criminal Law by *Judge John Copertino* (ISBN 0-87526-201-5)	$ 44.95
☐ New York Criminal Law Handbook [Softcover or Looseleaf] (ISBN 0-87526-309-7)	$ 24.95
☐ New York Criminal Procedure Law [Softcover or Looseleaf] (ISBN 0-87526-138-8)	$ 6.95
☐ New York Criminal Procedure Law DiskLaw™ on CD-ROM (ISBN 0-87526-457-3)	$ 19.95
☐ New York Criminal Procedure Law Questions & Answers (ISBN 0-87526-314-3)	$ 12.95
☐ New York Defense of Justification (Penal Law - Article 35 Review) (ISBN 0-87526-331-5)	$ 4.95
☐ New York *Gitlitz* on Divorces and Annulments (ISBN 0-87526-258-9)	$ 44.95
☐ New York Environmental Conservation Law [Looseleaf] (ISBN 0-87526-255-4)	$ 21.95
☐ New York Environmental Conservation Law [Softcover] (ISBN 0-87526-255-4)	$ 14.95
☐ New York Estates, Powers & Trusts Law (ISBN 0-87526-140-X)	$ 9.95
☐ New York E.P.T.L. & S.C.P.A. [Softcover or Looseleaf] (ISBN 0-87526-342-9)	$ 21.95
☐ New York E.P.T.L. & S.C.P.A. DiskLaw™ on CD-ROM (ISBN 0-87526-467-0)	$ 49.95*
☐ New York *Canudo* on Evidence Laws by *Gary Shaw* (ISBN 0-87526-175-2)	$ 39.95
☐ New York Family Law DiskLaw™ on CD-ROM (ISBN 0-87526-469-7)	$ 49.95*
☐ New York Family Law Handbook [Softcover or Looseleaf] (ISBN 0-87526-374-7)	$ 21.95
☐ New York Identification Law by *Miriam Hibel* [Softcover or Looseleaf] (ISBN 0-87526-533-2)	$ 44.95
☐ New York Insurance Law [Softcover] (ISBN 0-87526-539-1)	$ 19.95
☐ New York Landlord & Tenant Handbook (ISBN 0-87526-311-9)	$ 39.95
☐ New York Law Digest (ISBN 0-87526-252-X)	$ 14.95
☐ New York Law Enforcement Handbook (ISBN 0-87526-510-3)	$ 6.95
☐ New York Legal Forms and Procedures Handbook (ISBN 0-87526-362-3)	$ 49.95
☐ New York Legal Forms and Procedures DiskLaw™ on CD-ROM (ISBN 0-87526-512-X)	$ 99.00**
☐ New York Manual for Police (☐ Softcover ☐ Looseleaf ☐ CD-ROM) (ISBN 0-87526-570-7)	$ 29.95**
☐ New York Marriage Certificate [Softcover] (ISBN 0-87526-328-3)	$ 4.00
☐ New York Multiple Dwelling Law (ISBN 0-87526-285-6)	$ 16.95
☐ New York Penal Law [Softcover or Looseleaf] (ISBN 0-87526-145-0)	$ 6.95
☐ New York Penal Law, C.P.L. & V.T.L. DiskLaw™ on CD-ROM (ISBN 0-87526-446-8)	$ 49.95*
☐ New York Penal Law DiskLaw™ on CD-ROM (ISBN 0-87526-458-1)	$ 19.95
☐ New York Penal Law Pocket Slide Rule (ISBN 0-87526-287-2)	$ 6.00
☐ New York Penal Law & Criminal Procedure Law (ISBN 0-87526-326-7)	$ 9.95
☐ New York Penal Law Questions & Answers (ISBN 0-87526-313-5)	$ 12.95
☐ New York Practical Tips for Law Enforcement by *Barry Kamins* (ISBN 0-87526-423-9)	$ 5.95
☐ New York Real Property Law DiskLaw™ on CD-ROM (ISBN 0-87526-475-1)	$ 49.95*
☐ New York Real Property Law Handbook [Softcover or Looseleaf] (ISBN 0-87526-340-2)	$ 24.95
☐ New York Search & Seizure by *Barry Kamins* [Softcover or Looseleaf] (ISBN 0-87526-383-6)	$ 44.95
☐ New York Search & Seizure on CD-ROM (ISBN 0-87526-562-6)	$ 99.00
☐ New York Search & Seizure for Law Enforcement by *Barry Kamins* (ISBN 0-87526-430-1)	$ 9.95
☐ New York Security Officer Training Manual by *Lenahan & Blanchfield* [Softcover] (ISBN 0-87526-425-5)	$ 12.95
☐ New York Small Claims Guide [Softcover] (ISBN 0-87526-327-5)	$ 5.95
☐ New York Surrogate's Court Procedure Act (ISBN 0-87526-129-9)	$ 10.95
☐ New York Town Law (ISBN 0-87526-303-8)	$ 17.95
☐ New York Understanding the Penal Law by *Richard C. Moriarty* (ISBN 0-87526-416-6)	$ 25.95
☐ New York Vehicle & Traffic Law [Softcover or Looseleaf] (ISBN 0-87526-373-9)	$ 9.95
☐ New York Vehicle & Traffic Law DiskLaw™ on CD-ROM (ISBN 0-87526-459-X)	$ 29.95
☐ New York Vehicle & Traffic Law with NYC Traffic Rules [Softcover] (ISBN 0-87526-545-6)	$ 15.95
☐ New York Vehicle & Traffic Law Flip Code™ (ISBN 0-87526-333-X)	$ 8.95
☐ New York Vehicle & Traffic Law Pocket Slide Rule (ISBN 0-87526-288-1)	$ 6.00
☐ New York Village Law (ISBN 0-87526-308-9)	$ 15.95
☐ New York *Bloom* on Wills Laws by *Maureen O'Brien* (ISBN 0-87526-404-2)	$ 34.95

(continued)

☐ New York Workers' Compensation Law Handbook (ISBN 0-87526-380-1) .... $ 39.95
☐ Assessment Center Handbook *by Brian T. Page* [Softcover] (ISBN 0-87526-429-8) .... $ 21.95
☐ Commercial Law Handbook (ISBN 0-87526-312-7) .... $ 24.95
☐ Contemporary Crim. Procedure *by Larry E. Holtz* [Softcover or Looseleaf] (ISBN 0-87526-365-8) .... $ 44.95
☐ Criminal Evidence For Law Enforcement (3rd Ed.) *by Larry E. Holtz* [Looseleaf] (ISBN 0-87526-393-3) .... $ 29.95
☐ Criminal Justice Terms—Bilingual Dictionary (*English/Spanish*) [Softcover or Looseleaf] (ISBN 0-87526-379-8) ...... $ 24.95
☐ Criminal Laws & Procedure—All 50 states and Federal on CD-ROM—*DiskLaw*™ (ISBN 0-87526-544-8) .... $ 499.00**
☐ Customs Law Handbook (ISBN 0-87526-343-7) .... $ 29.00
☐ Defensive Tactics for Law Enforcement *by R. A. Flesch* [Softcover] (ISBN 0-87526-421-2) .... $ 25.95
☐ Dictionary of Criminal Justice Terms [Softcover] (ISBN 0-87526-276-7) .... $ 14.95
☐ Disabled Offenders (Stop, Search, and Arrest) *by Bolin, Flesch, and Funk* [Softcover] (ISBN 0-87526-542-1) .... $ 29.95
☐ Drug Laws — All 50 states and Federal on CD-ROM — *DiskLaw*™ (ISBN 0-87526-514-6) .... $ 249.00**
☐ DRUGS and the LAW (2nd Ed.) *by G. Miller* [Softcover] (ISBN 0-87526-398-4) .... $ 44.95
☐ Federal Bankruptcy Handbook [Softcover or Looseleaf] (ISBN 0-87526-245-7) .... $ 25.00
☐ Federal Civil Procedure Handbook [Softcover or Looseleaf] (ISBN 0-87526-301-1) .... $ 25.00
☐ Federal Criminal Law Handbook [Softcover or Looseleaf] (ISBN 0-87526-315-1) .... $ 25.00
☐ Federal Rules of Evidence (ISBN 0-87526-207-4) .... $ 15.95
☐ Fire Problem and its Solution (2nd Ed.) *by Charles V. Walsh* [Softcover] (ISBN 0-87526-394-1) .... $ 34.95
☐ Firearms Laws — All 50 states and Federal on CD-ROM — *DiskLaw*™ (ISBN 0-87526-515-4) .... $ 349.00**
☐ Graphing And Charting, Simplified *by Henry J. Mulhearn* [Softcover] (ISBN 0-87526-221-X) .... $ 12.95
☐ Immigration Terms—Bilingual Dictionary (*English/Spanish*) [Softcover or Looseleaf] (ISBN 0-87526-541-3) .... $ 24.95
☐ Investigative & Operational Report Writing (3rd Ed.) *by Larry E. Holtz* [Softcover] (ISBN 0-87526-372-0) .... $ 11.95
☐ Juvenile & Domestic Relations Terms—Bilingual Dictionary (*English/Spanish*) [Softcover or Looseleaf] (ISBN 0-87526-540-5) .... $ 24.95
☐ Knife Defense for Law Enforcement *by R. A. Flesch* [Softcover] (ISBN 0-87526-422-0) .... $ 17.95
☐ License Plate Book *with Drivers Licenses* [Softcover] (ISBN 1-886777-012) .... $ 16.95
☐ Management & Supervision of Law Enforcement Personnel (2nd Edition) [Softcover] (ISBN 0-87526-428-X) .... $ 34.95
☐ Necessary Elements [Softcover] (ISBN 0-87526-242-2) .... $ 6.00
☐ Pertinent Commercial Statutes (ISBN 0-87526-293-7) .... $ 14.95
☐ Plate Tracer *by Thomson C. Murray* — *DiskLaw*™ on CD-ROM .... $ 49.95
☐ Police Science Fundamentals *by Henry J. Mulhearn* [Softcover] (ISBN 0-87526-160-4) .... $ 14.95
☐ Promotional Test Questions *by D. DelBagno* [Softcover] (ISBN 0-87526-381-X) .... $ 25.95
☐ School Violence: Law Enforcement Use of Force (Reasonable and Deadly) *by Bolin, Funk, Flesch, and Osborne* (ISBN 0-87526-553-7) .... $ 24.95
☐ Security Investigation *by Smith and Celano* [Softcover] (ISBN 0-87526-513-8) .... $ 19.95
☐ Spanish for Law Enforcement *w/ cassette (Field & Reference FlipCode™)* (*English/Spanish*) (ISBN 0-87526-427-1) ...... $ 29.95
☐ Stress Mgmt. for Law Enf. (Behind the Shield: Combating Trauma) *by Pranzo and Pranzo* [Softcover] (ISBN 0-87526-532-4) .. $ 24.95
☐ Supervision Handbook *by Mario J. Ferrari* [Softcover] (ISBN 0-87526-378-X) .... $ 17.95
☐ Torts *by Theodore Schussler* [Softcover] (ISBN 0-87526-166-3) .... $ 10.00
☐ Uniform Commercial Code (8th Ed.) [Softcover or Looseleaf] (ISBN 0-87526-251-1) .... $ 21.95
☐ United States Code Unannotated™ (USCU™) — *DiskLaw*™ on CD-ROM .... $ 99.00**
☐ Use of Force for Law Enforcement Field and Reference FlipCode (ISBN 0-87526-554-5) .... $ 15.95
☐ Vehicle Laws — All 50 states and Federal on CD-ROM — *DiskLaw*™ (ISBN 0-87526-516-2) .... $ 499.00**

     Subtotal $ ....
     Add shipping & handling $ ....
     Add New York sales tax where applicable $ ....
     Total $ ....

SHIPPING CHARGES IN THE U.S.

$5.00 for the first item, $4.00 for the second item, and $3.00 for each additional item. Alaska, Hawaii and Puerto Rico—orders are shipped 2nd Day Air and charged current 2nd Day Air rates in addition to above charges unless otherwise requested. Add $25 per each set of Consolidated Laws of New York, looseleaf or softcover.

SHIPPING CHARGES OUTSIDE THE U.S.

FPO, APO, Canada and international countries are shipped via surface mail—$9.00 per item. Add $80 for each set of Consolidated Laws of New York.

For complete listings, see our new catalogue.
*See reverse side for multiple-user/network prices for Gould's *DiskLaw*™ products.
**Contact your Gould representative for multiple-user/network prices for Gould's *DiskLaw*™ products
Unless otherwise noted, publications are looseleaf editions.
National publications list is available separately.

Please ship us the items we have checked. We understand that upon purchasing we become subscribers and will be notified by subscription invoice of the next available update, except for electronic products and authored titles which are auto-ship.
We will notify you in writing if we wish to cancel.

Quantity discounts available • Prices subject to change without notice • Minimum required for Billing or Charging is $15.00

☐ We have enclosed our check or money order in the amount of $ _____, including sales tax (where applicable) and shipping.
☐ Please send us a catalog and price listing for future ordering.   ☐ Please send us information on GouldLaw™ via the Internet.
Charge to (circle one): MasterCard   VISA   AmEx   Authorized Signature (REQUIRED) _____

Card #   Exp. Date

Tel. Number   Department/Agency

Name (Please print)

Street Address (No P.O. Boxes, please)   Apt./Suite #

City   State   Zip Code

E-mail address _____

GOULD PUBLICATIONS • GOULDLAW™

199/300 State Street, Binghamton, NY 13901-2782 • Fax: (607) 723-4285 • Tel: (800) 847-6502 • E-mail: info@gouldlaw.com
Want more information? Point your browser to www.gouldlaw.com
Sample software and Search Engine • Complete Catalog • Tables of Contents for each publication • Links and Legal Resources
For Quick Credit Card Purchases, try our Internet Shopping Cart.

Gould Publications
Price List and Order Form

- ☐ Assessment Center Handbook *by Brian T. Page* [Softcover] (ISBN 0-87526-429-8) .... $ 21.95
- ☐ California Evidence Code [Softcover] (ISBN 0-87526-561-8) .... $ 5.95
- ☐ California Fish and Game Code (ISBN 0-87526-324-0) .... $ 24.95
- ☐ California Penal Code Handbook [Looseleaf] (ISBN 0-87526-268-6) .... $ 24.95
- ☐ California Penal Code Handbook [Softcover] (ISBN 0-87526-268-6) .... $ 21.95
- ☐ California Penal Code Pocket Slide Rule (ISBN 0-87526-291-0) .... $ 6.00
- ☐ California Vehicle Code [Looseleaf] (ISBN 0-87526-269-4) .... $ 18.95
- ☐ California Vehicle Code [Softcover] (ISBN 0-87526-269-4) .... $ 15.95
- ☐ California Vehicle Code Pocket Slide Rule (ISBN 0-87526-292-9) .... $ 6.00
- ☐ Chicago Municipal Code Handbook (ISBN 0-87526-264-3) .... $ 24.95
- ☐ Commercial Law Handbook (ISBN 0-87526-312-7) .... $ 24.95
- ☐ Confession Standards *by Nathan R. Sobel* [Hardcover] (ISBN 0-87526-016-0) .... $ 9.95
- ☐ Connecticut Criminal Laws (ISBN 0-87526-229-5) .... $ 9.95
- ☐ Connecticut Criminal & Motor Vehicle Laws [Looseleaf] (0-87526-509-x) .... $ 11.95
- ☐ Connecticut Law Enforcement Handbook [Softcover or Looseleaf] (ISBN 0-87526-353-4) .... $ 7.95
- ☐ Connecticut Motor Vehicle Laws (ISBN 0-87526-391-7) .... $ 9.95
- ☐ Court Decisions for Law Enforcement *(aka Contemp. Crim. Proc.) by Larry E. Holtz* [Softcover or Looseleaf] (ISBN 0-87526-365-8) .... $ 44.95
- ☐ Criminal Evidence (3rd Ed.) *by Larry E. Holtz* (ISBN 0-87526-393-3) .... $ 29.95
- ☐ Criminal Justice Terms—Bilingual Dictionary *(English/Spanish)* [Softcover or Looseleaf] (ISBN 0-87526-379-8) .... $ 24.95
- ☐ Criminal Laws and Procedure — All 50 states and Federal on CD-ROM—DiskLaw™ (ISBN 0-87526-544-8) .... $ 499.00*
- ☐ Customs Law Handbook (ISBN 0-87526-343-7) .... $ 29.00
- ☐ Defensive Tactics for Law Enforcement *by R. A. Flesch* [Softcover] (ISBN 0-87526-421-2) .... $ 25.95
- ☐ Dictionary of Criminal Justice Terms [Softcover] (ISBN 0-87526-276-7) .... $ 14.95
- ☐ Disabled Offenders (Stop, Search, and Arrest) *by Bolin, Flesch and Funk* [Looseleaf] (ISBN 0-87526-542-1) .... $ 29.95
- ☐ District of Columbia Criminal Law & Motor Vehicle Handbook [Softcover or Looseleaf] (ISBN 1-882476-07-7) .... $ 19.95
- ☐ Drug Laws — All 50 states and Federal on CD-ROM — DiskLaw™ (ISBN 0-87526-514-6) .... $ 249.00*
- ☐ DRUGS and the LAW—Detection, Recognition & Investigation (2nd Ed.) *by Miller* [Softcover] (ISBN 0-87526-398-4) .... $ 44.95
- ☐ Federal Bankruptcy Handbook [Softcover or Looseleaf] (ISBN 0-87526-245-7) .... $ 25.00
- ☐ Federal Civil Procedure Handbook [Softcover or Looseleaf] (ISBN 0-87526-301-1) .... $ 25.00
- ☐ Federal Criminal Law Handbook [Softcover or Looseleaf] (ISBN 0-87526-315-1) .... $ 25.00
- ☐ Federal Rules of Evidence (ISBN 0-87526-207-4) .... $ 15.00
- ☐ Fire Problem and Its Solution (2nd Ed.) *by Charles V. Walsh* [Softcover] (ISBN 0-87526-394-1) .... $ 34.95
- ☐ Firearms Laws — All 50 states and Federal on CD-ROM — DiskLaw™ (ISBN 0-87526-515-4) .... $ 349.00*
- ☐ Florida Criminal Jury Instructions Handbook [Softcover] (ISBN 0-87526-552-9) .... $ 21.95
- ☐ Florida Criminal Law & Motor Vehicle Handbook [Looseleaf] (ISBN 0-87526-375-5) .... $ 24.95
- ☐ Florida Criminal Law & Motor Vehicle Handbook [Softcover] (ISBN 0-87526-375-5) .... $ 22.95
- ☐ Florida Criminal Laws (ISBN 0-87526-188-4) .... $ 16.95
- ☐ Florida Criminal Laws Pocket Slide Rule (ISBN 0-87526-274-0) .... $ 6.00
- ☐ Florida Motor Vehicle Laws (ISBN 0-87526-256-2) .... $ 16.95
- ☐ Florida Motor Vehicle Laws Pocket Slide Rule (ISBN 0-87526-280-5) .... $ 6.00
- ☐ Florida Security Officer's Handbook *by Rex Stevenson III* [Softcover] (ISBN 0-87526-432-8) .... $ 15.95
- ☐ Georgia Conservation Law Handbook (ISBN 1-882476-06-9) .... $ 28.00
- ☐ Georgia Criminal Law & Motor Vehicle Handbook (ISBN 1-882476-02-6) .... $ 21.95
- ☐ Georgia Security Officer's Handbook *by Rex Stevenson III* [Softcover] (ISBN 0-87526-537-5) .... $ 15.95
- ☐ Graphing And Charting, Simplified *by Henry J. Mulhearn* [Softcover] (ISBN 0-87526-221-X) .... $ 12.95
- ☐ Illinois Compiled Statutes Unannotated (ICSU™) on CD-ROM (ISBN 0-87526-431-X) .... $ 129.00*
- ☐ Illinois Conservation Law (ISBN 0-87526-354-2) .... $ 21.95
- ☐ Illinois Criminal Law & Traffic Law Manual [Softcover or Looseleaf] (ISBN 0-87526-414-X) .... $ 31.95
- ☐ Illinois Criminal Law & Procedure Handbook [Softcover or Looseleaf] (ISBN 0-87526-199-X) .... $ 19.95
- ☐ Illinois Criminal Law & Procedure Pocket Slide Rule (ISBN 0-87526-270-8) .... $ 6.00
- ☐ Illinois Vehicle Code [Softcover or Looseleaf] (ISBN 0-87526-259-7) .... $ 19.95
- ☐ Illinois Vehicle Code Pocket Slide Rule (ISBN 0-87526-289-8) .... $ 6.00
- ☐ Immigration Terms—Bilingual Dictionary *(English/Spanish)* [Looseleaf or Softcover] (ISBN 0-87526-541-3) .... $ 24.95
- ☐ Indiana Criminal Law & Motor Vehicle Handbook [Softcover or Looseleaf] (ISBN 0-87526-366-6) .... $ 19.95
- ☐ Investigative & Operational Report Writing (3rd Ed.) *by Larry E. Holtz* [Softcover] (ISBN 0-87526-372-0) .... $ 11.95
- ☐ Juvenile & Domestic Relations Terms—Bilingual Dictionary *(Eng./Span.)* [Looseleaf or Softcover] (ISBN 0-87526-540-5) .... $ 24.95
- ☐ Knife Defense for Law Enforcement *by R. A. Flesch* [Softcover] (ISBN 0-87526-422-0) .... $ 17.95
- ☐ License Plate Book *includes Drivers Licenses* [Softcover] (ISBN 1-886777-012) .... $ 16.95
- ☐ Louisiana Criminal Law & Motor Vehicle Handbook [Softcover or Looseleaf] (ISBN 0-87526-367-4) .... $ 24.95
- ☐ Management & Supervision of Law Enforcement Personnel [Softcover] (ISBN 0-87526-428-X) .... $ 34.95
- ☐ Management & Supervision of Law Enforcement Personnel on CD-ROM—DiskLaw™ (ISBN 0-87526-565-0) .... $ 69.95
- ☐ Maryland Criminal Law & Motor Vehicle Handbook [Softcover or Looseleaf] (ISBN 1-882476-04-2) .... $ 21.95
- ☐ Massachusetts Criminal Law & Procedure (ISBN 0-87526-320-8) .... $ 21.95
- ☐ Massachusetts Criminal Law & Procedure Pocket Slide Rule (ISBN 0-87526-275-9) .... $ 6.00
- ☐ Massachusetts Environmental Law Handbook (ISBN 0-87526-426-3) .... $ 34.95
- ☐ Massachusetts Motor Vehicle & Traffic Laws (ISBN 0-87526-231-7) .... $ 21.95
- ☐ Massachusetts Motor Vehicle & Traffic Laws Flip Code™ (ISBN 0-87526-550-2) .... $ 8.95
- ☐ Michigan Motor Vehicle Laws with Uniform Traffic Code (ISBN 0-87526-253-8) .... $ 17.95
- ☐ Michigan Motor Vehicle Laws Pocket Slide Rule (ISBN 0-87526-282-1) .... $ 6.00
- ☐ Michigan Penal Code (ISBN 0-87526-254-6) .... $ 17.95
- ☐ Michigan Penal Code and Motor Vehicle Handbook including Uniform Traffic Code [Softcover] (ISBN 0-87526-557-X) .... $ 29.95
- ☐ Michigan Penal Code Pocket Slide Rule (ISBN 0-87526-286-4) .... $ 6.00
- ☐ Michigan Probate Code (ISBN 0-87526-306-2) .... $ 16.00
- ☐ New Jersey Civil Practice and Court Rules (ISBN 0-87526-299-6) .... $ 21.95
- ☐ New Jersey *Contemporary* Criminal Procedure (2 Volumes) *by Larry E. Holtz* [Softcover] (ISBN 0-87526-369-0) .... $ 79.95
- ☐ New Jersey *Contemporary* Criminal Procedure (2 Volumes) on CD-ROM *by Larry E. Holtz* (ISBN 0-87526-534-0) .... $ 129.95
- ☐ New Jersey Criminal Justice Code (ISBN 0-87526-024-1) .... $ 18.95
- ☐ New Jersey Criminal Justice Code Pocket Slide Rule (ISBN 0-87526-272-4) .... $ 6.00
- ☐ New Jersey Criminal Law and Motor Vehicle Handbook [Softcover] (ISBN 0-87526-371-2) .... $ 29.95
- ☐ New Jersey Law Enforcement Handbook (2 Volumes) *by Larry E. Holtz* (ISBN 0-87526-325-9) .... $ 79.95
- ☐ New Jersey Law Enforcement Handbook on CD-ROM (2 Volumes) *by Larry E. Holtz* (ISBN 0-87526-534-0) .... $ 129.95

Effective June 21, 2000

(continued)

☐ New Jersey Motor Vehicle & Traffic Laws (ISBN 0-87526-232-5) .... $ 18.95
☐ New Jersey Motor Vehicle & Traffic Laws [Softcover] (ISBN 0-87526-232-5) .... $ 14.95
☐ New Jersey Motor Vehicle & Traffic Laws Pocket Slide Rule (ISBN 0-87526-284-8) .... $ 6.00
☐ New York Consolidated Laws (9-volume set) [☐Softcover ☐Looseleaf ☐CD-ROM] .... $ 179.00*
☐ New York Consolidated Laws Legal Assistant Edition (ISBN 0-87526-360-2) .... $ 49.95
☐ North Carolina Criminal Law & Motor Vehicle Handbook [Softcover] (ISBN 1-882476-00-X) .... $ 21.95
☐ Ohio Criminal Code (ISBN 0-87526-202-3) .... $ 17.95
☐ Ohio Criminal Code Pocket Slide Rule (ISBN 0-87526-273-2) .... $ 6.00
☐ Ohio Criminal Law & Motor Vehicle Handbook [Softcover or Looseleaf] (ISBN 0-87526-386-0) .... $ 23.00
☐ Ohio Motor Vehicle Laws (ISBN 0-87526-257-0) .... $ 17.95
☐ Ohio Motor Vehicle Laws Pocket Slide Rule (ISBN 0-87526-283-X) .... $ 6.00
☐ Pennsylvania *Contemporary* Criminal Procedure by Larry E. Holtz [Softcover] (ISBN 0-87526-370-4) ... $ 49.95
☐ Pennsylvania Crimes Code (ISBN 0-87526-216-3) .... $ 21.95
☐ Pennsylvania Crimes Code, Vehicle Law, & Related Statutes and Rules Handbook [Softcover] (ISBN 0-87526-559-6) ... $ 39.95
☐ Pennsylvania Crimes Code Flip Code™ (ISBN 0-87526-387-9) .... $ 8.95
☐ Pennsylvania Criminal Law Digest (ISBN 0-87526-237-6) .... $ 21.95
☐ Pennsylvania Judiciary and Judicial Procedure (Title 42) (ISBN 0-87526-295-3) .... $ 21.95
☐ Pennsylvania Law Enforcement Handbook by Larry E. Holtz (ISBN 0-87526-355-0) .... $ 49.95
☐ Pennsylvania Rules of Civil Procedure (Title 231) (ISBN 0-87526-300-3) .... $ 18.95
☐ Pennsylvania Vehicles Law (ISBN 0-87526-233-3) .... $ 21.95
☐ Pennsylvania Vehicles Law Flip Code™ (ISBN 0-87526-388-7) .... $ 8.95
☐ Pertinent Commercial Statutes (ISBN 0-87526-293-7) .... $ 14.95
☐ Plate Tracer by *Thomson C. Murray* [CD-ROM] .... $ 49.95
☐ Police Science Fundamentals by Henry J. Mulhearn [Softcover] (ISBN 0-87526-160-4) .... $ 14.95
☐ Promotional Test Questions by D. DelBagno [Softcover] (ISBN 0-87526-381-X) .... $ 25.95
☐ School Violence: Law Enforcement Use of Force (Reasonable and Deadly) by Bolin, Funk, Fleech and Osborne (ISBN 0-87526-553-7) ... $ 24.95
☐ Security Investigation by *Smith and Celano* [Softcover] (ISBN 0-87526-513-8) .... $ 19.95
☐ South Carolina Criminal Law & Motor Vehicle Handbook [Softcover or Looseleaf] (ISBN 1-882476-05-0) ... $ 24.95
☐ Spanish for Law Enforcement (Field & Reference FlipCode™) (*English/Spanish w/cassette*) (ISBN 0-87526-427-1) ... $ 29.95
☐ Stress Management for Law Enf. (Behind the Shield: Combating Trauma) by Pranzo & Pranzo [Softcover] (ISBN 0-87526-532-4) ... $ 24.95
☐ Supervision Handbook by Mario J. Ferrari [Softcover] (ISBN 0-87526-378-X) .... $ 17.95
☐ Texas *Contemporary* Criminal Procedure by Holtz & Spencer [Softcover] (ISBN 0-9629210-4-1) .... $ 34.95
☐ Texas Criminal Law & Motor Vehicle Handbook [Looseleaf] (ISBN 0-9629210-0-9) .... $ 26.95
☐ Texas Criminal Law & Motor Vehicle Handbook [Softcover] (ISBN 0-9629210-0-9) .... $ 22.95
☐ Texas Criminal Laws [Softcover] (ISBN 0-9629210-8-4) .... $ 13.95
☐ Texas Law Enforcement Handbook by Holtz & Spencer [Softcover] (ISBN 0-9629210-5-X) .... $ 34.95
☐ Texas Law Enforcement on CD-ROM—*DiskLaw™* by Holtz & Spencer (ISBN 0-9629210-9-2) .... $ 99.95*
☐ Texas Penal Code Flip Code™ (ISBN 0-9629210-3-3) .... $ 9.95
☐ Texas Traffic Laws [Softcover] (ISBN 0-9629210-7-6) .... $ 11.95
☐ Texas Vehicle Laws Flip Code™ (ISBN 0-9629210-2-5) .... $ 9.95
☐ Uniform Commercial Code [Softcover or Looseleaf] (ISBN 0-87526-251-1) .... $ 21.95
☐ United States Code Unannotated™ (USCU™) on CD-ROM (ISBN 0-87526-454-9) .... $ 99.00*
☐ Use of Force for Law Enforcement Field and Reference FlipCode™ (ISBN 0-87526-554-5) .... $ 15.95
☐ Vehicle Laws — All 50 states and Federal on CD-ROM — *DiskLaw™* (ISBN 0-87526-516-2) .... $ 499.00*
☐ Virginia Criminal Law & Motor Vehicle Handbook [Softcover or Looseleaf] (ISBN 1-882476-01-8) ..... $ 21.95
☐ Virginia Search and Seizure for Law Enforcement Officers by Russell N. Allen (ISBN 0-87526-551-0) ... $ 19.95
☐ Wyoming Criminal Law & Motor Vehicle Handbook (ISBN 0-87526-368-2) .... $ 21.95

SHIPPING CHARGES IN THE U.S.
$5.00 for the first item, $4.00 for the second item; and $3.00 for each additional item. Alaska, Hawaii and Puerto Rico — orders are shipped 2nd Day Air and charged current 2nd Day Air rates in addition to above charges unless otherwise requested. Add $25 per each set of Consolidated Laws of New York, looseleaf or softcover.

SHIPPING CHARGES OUTSIDE THE U.S.
FPO, APO, Canada and international countries are shipped via surface mail — $9.00 per item. Add $80 for each set of Consolidated Laws of New York, looseleaf or softcover.

Subtotal $ ....
Add shipping & handling $ ....
Add Fla., N.Y. or Texas sales tax where applicable $ ....
Total $ ....

For complete listings, see our new catalogue.
*Contact your Gould representative for multiple-user/network prices for Gould's *DiskLaw™* products
Unless otherwise noted, publications are looseleaf editions.
New York publications list is available separately.

Please ship us the items we have checked. We understand that upon purchasing we become subscribers and will be notified by subscription invoice of the next available update, except for electronic products and authored titles which are auto-ship. We will notify you in writing if we wish to cancel.

Quantity discounts available • Prices subject to change without notice • Minimum required for Billing or Charging is $15.00

☐ We have enclosed our check or money order in the amount of $ _____, including sales tax (where applicable) and shipping.
☐ Please send us a catalog and price listing for future ordering.   ☐ Please send us information on GouldLaw™ via the Internet.
Charge to (circle one): MasterCard   VISA   AmEx   Authorized Signature (REQUIRED) _____

Card # _____   Exp. Date _____

Tel. Number _____   Department/Agency _____

Name (Please print) _____

Street Address (No P.O. Boxes, please) _____   Apt./Suite # _____

City _____   State _____   Zip Code _____

E-mail address _____

GOULD PUBLICATIONS, INC. • GOULDLAW™
1333 North US Highway 17-92, Longwood, FL 32750-3724 • Fax: (407) 695-2906 • Tel: (407) 695-9500 • E-mail: info@gouldlaw.com

Want more information? Point your browser to www.gouldlaw.com
Sample software and Search Engine • Complete Catalog • Tables of Contents for each publication • Links and Legal Resources
For Quick Credit Card Purchases, try our Internet Shopping Cart.